Richard Cohen

GAY
CHILDREN

A Plan for Family Healing

STRAIGHT
PARENTS

IVP Books
An imprint of InterVarsity Press
Downers Grove, Illinois

InterVarsity Press
P.O. Box 1400, Downers Grove, IL 60515-1426
World Wide Web: www.ivpress.com
E-mail: email@ivpress.com

InterVarsity Press® is the book-publishing division of InterVarsity Christian Fellowship/USA®, a student movement active on campus at hundreds of universities, colleges and schools of nursing in the United States of America, and a member movement of the International Fellowship of Evangelical Students. For information about local and regional activities, write Public Relations Dept., InterVarsity Christian Fellowship/USA, 6400 Schroeder Rd., P.O. Box 7895, Madison, WI 53707-7895, or visit the IVCF website at <www.intervarsity.org>.

All Scripture quotations, unless otherwise indicated, are taken from the Holy Bible, New International Version®. NIV®. *Copyright ©1973, 1978, 1984 by International Bible Society. Used by permission of Zondervan Publishing House. All rights reserved.*

All names have been changed to protect the confidentiality of those who willingly shared their stories for the benefit of others.

Design: Cindy Kiple
Images: photo: Micah Weber/iStockphoto.com
    family photograph: Trinette Reed/Brand X Pictures/jupiterimages.com

ISBN 978-0-8308-3437-2

Printed in the United States of America ∞

Library of Congress Cataloging-in-Publication Data

Cohen, Richard, 1952 Oct. 15-
  Gay children, straight parents: a plan for family healing / Richard
Cohen.
    p. cm.
Includes bibliographical references.
ISBN 978-0-8308-3437-2 (pbk.: alk. paper)
  1. Parent and child—Religious aspects—Christianity. 2. Sexual
orientation. I. Title.
BV4529.C57 2007
261.8'3576—dc22

                                                              2007011187

| P | 19 | 18 | 17 | 16 | 15 | 14 | 13 | 12 | 11 | 10 | 9 | 8 | 7 | 6 | 5 | 4 |
| Y | 23 | 22 | 21 | 20 | 19 | 18 | 17 | 16 | 15 | 14 | 13 | 12 | 11 | | | | |

I dedicate this book to . . .

God, my source, my comfort, my love.

Jae Sook, my loving, steadfast and amazing wife.

My prodigal son, Jarish. I love you forever.

My precious Jessica. You are so beautiful. Keep evolving.

My powerful Alfred. You are my sunshine.

My new daughter, Yi Hwa. Thank you for joining our family.

All who prayed for and supported this endeavor.
Without you, this book would not have been written.

All the parents who have participated in the teleconferencing classes.
You taught me so much.

My dear friends John, Hilde, Mel, Bob, Lee, Jim and Russell.
Your love sustains me.

Pastor Ron and Brenda Crawford and New Vision Church.
We stand together.

Contents

Acknowledgments

Thanks to Carl and Regina Griggs for the sanctuary by the Bay to write in peace! Thanks for your enduring friendship.

Thanks to Arthur and Jane Goldberg for your friendship, support and excellent ideas to improve this and other works. You're my true brother and sister.

Thanks to my wonderful editor and coach, Gary Deddo, and the staff at InterVarsity Press for brilliantly bringing this book to life.

Thanks to Stuart, Sam, Bonnie, Mary, Tom, Mark, Manny, Lise and others for sharing your stories of victory and hope.

Thanks to Christoph, Burt, Jese, Mel, Barbara and Nancy for your invaluable assistance.

Thanks to Manny and Lise for your loving hearts and faithful support. You are dear friends.

Thanks to Scott and Dori—you were the inspiration for this book.

Darkness cannot drive out darkness;
only light can do that.
Hate cannot drive out hate;
only love can do that.

—Martin Luther King Jr.

Introduction

Never give up! Those three words have been a driving force throughout my life. So many times, when I was attempting to understand and overcome my unwanted same-sex attractions (SSA),[1] I wanted to give up. But no matter how many times I fell down, I kept getting up again. I never quit. Finally, against all odds, I came out straight. Today I have been married to my beautiful wife, Jae Sook, for twenty-five years, and we have three incredible children.

After overcoming my own SSA, I wanted to help others who struggle with the same issues. I felt called by God to return to school and obtain an education in counseling. I graduated from Antioch University (Seattle campus) in 1990 with a Master of Arts degree in counseling psychology and then established the International Healing Foundation. Thus began my professional life as a psychotherapist, public speaker and writer addressing the causes and treatment of unwanted SSA.

As a professional psychotherapist as well as a former homosexual, I have personally assisted hundreds of men and women in the process of changing their orientation from homosexual to heterosexual. In over a hundred healing seminars throughout the United States and Europe, I have been able to help thousands find freedom from unwanted same-sex attraction. On college campuses and at therapeutic and religious conferences, I have lectured about the causes and treatment of homosexuality.

Along with helping men and women heal from unwanted SSA, I have also listened to the heartaches of hundreds of parents over the past seventeen years:

---

[1] I will use *SSA* throughout the book to denote same-sex attraction.

- "What can we do?"
- "Why did this happen?"
- "Our son knows we are strong believers in Christ, and yet he is in complete rebellion."
- "I'm afraid to tell my pastor or friends for fear they will judge us and our daughter."
- "All we hear in our church are negative things about homosexuals."
- "In the Orthodox Jewish community, it would be very punishing if people found out that our son is gay."

This book is the result of my life's journey out of homosexuality and the seventeen years of clinical experience that followed. It represents weeks, months and years of coaching and counseling hundreds of families and friends to help their loved ones realize their true gender identity and experience their heterosexual potential. In the pages that follow, I will share with you specific principles about how to help loved ones who struggle with SSA. This plan, which will help them, requires your discipline and diligence. But the wonderful by-product is that you too will be transformed and will experience greater love than you ever imagined. In the meantime, you will be encouraged as you read the many success stories.

You will need encouragement along the way because the journey is not easy. You will need tenacity, endurance and love beyond measure. This too I know personally and professionally, because my wife and I once had a prodigal son. The principles that I will describe don't apply just to SSA; they apply to any loved one who is hurting and perhaps living in rebellion. My wife and I utilized all these skills with our oldest son, Jarish, whose story you will read about in the conclusion of this book. He did not suffer with SSA but was deeply wounded and sustained other problems as a result of our individual and marital conflicts.

Before my marriage, I had remained celibate for nine years. However, in the preceding years, I lived as an active homosexual man. Along the way, I experienced a religious conversion that helped me leave the "gay" life behind. But I never dealt with the root causes of my SSA. I simply repressed those desires and followed the advice of my elders: "Pray hard, and God will take away your homosexual feelings. Study God's Word, and you won't be burdened with those desires again. God will transform you, so don't worry about your feelings."

The worst advice of all was this: "Find the right woman and she'll straighten you out." Well, I did, she didn't, and the result was catastrophic. Completely confused, disappointed and frustrated, I went into therapy, desperately trying to figure out why I still had the same-sex attractions, which I did not want.

It took years to discover the causes of my SSA. It took even longer to heal from the wounds that created those desires in the first place. It was a messy process. Meanwhile I was working two jobs to support our family and pay for therapy. During that time, we had two children, Jarish and our daughter Jessica (our other son came along many years later). When Jarish was born, I had just begun my journey of healing, which ultimately led me out of homosexuality. As you might imagine, at that time I was highly ineffective as both husband and father.

To make matters worse, all this took place in the early 1980s, when there was little understanding about same-sex attractions and how to come out straight. Our family moved several times in pursuit of effective treatment, in search of professionals who were the most knowledgeable about SSA. Jarish and Jessica were, of course, uprooted every time we moved.

My process of healing was painful for the entire family. Jae Sook held on to God for dear life. I pleaded with her, "Please don't divorce me. I love God, I love you, and I love our children. I have to figure this out. Nobody has been able to help me thus far. Hold on, dear. I know that God will show us the way."

She and I both held on to God. I believed that he would eventually lead me out of the desert and into the promised land of my true heterosexuality and a healthy family life. It took many years and many failed attempts, but finally I broke through and found freedom from those unwanted desires.[2]

During those dark years, we were barely surviving, trying to claw our way out of hell and create the family of our dreams. In all the turmoil, Jarish was deeply hurt. Once I'd experienced my own personal healing, my wife and I immediately began to work on our relationship, a process that took several more years. Meanwhile our kids continued to be in pain. After our marriage improved, we worked hard to help Jarish and Jessica heal their wounds. And we all participated in counseling and family healing sessions.

But despite our efforts, Jarish had unresolved issues, and during high school he became angry and rebellious. Although he was not tempted by SSA, he was drawn into other behaviors that broke our hearts. Jae Sook and I tried to reach him, but he was extremely resistant. At times we made headway, but at other times he completely rejected us. We begged God to intervene. We fought with Jarish, we cried with him, we talked with him long into the night. Finally, miraculously, after many years, he broke through. Our prodigal son returned.

In the conclusion of this book, you'll read in Jarish's own words what he experienced during those years of agony. Today he is dedicated to our loving God, married to a wonderful woman and is working on an M.D./Ph.D. in medical school. It is his dream to pursue genetic research; he is committed to finding a cure for cancer.

Not only have I faced my own struggle with same-sex attraction, I have also wrestled with the pain of seeing a beloved child rebelling and

---

[2]You will find a more detailed description of my story in chapter one of *Coming Out Straight: Understanding and Healing Homosexuality*.

hurting himself. Therefore I can well understand the humbling journey of a parent whose child struggles with SSA. Based on my personal and professional experiences, I know I can help you and your child find the healing you seek. Impossible as it may seem at times, we are not alone in our battle for our children. Through God's grace and love, all things are possible.

How to Respond When a Loved One Has SSA

I know you must have been shocked when your child first "came out of the closet." Maybe you were completely taken by surprise. Or perhaps you'd had an inkling all along and your worst fears were realized. Whatever the circumstances surrounding the revelation, the parental response is usually the same: "How could this happen? I loved you with all my heart. I know I made mistakes, but God knows I tried my best." Maybe you blurted out all the wrong things at first. Or maybe you didn't say what you should have said.

Whatever happened, don't worry about the past. You can restore and improve your relationship with your SSA child. No matter how unlikely it may seem, be assured that he or she is hungry for your love, acceptance and approval.

It probably took your child years to disclose his or her hidden homosexual feelings. It was a long, lonely and painful journey that was made *without* you. Can you imagine what it must have been like for him in elementary, middle or high school to feel sexual attractions toward members of the same sex when all his peers were attracted to the opposite sex? How conflicted and confusing it must have been. And if your daughter grew up with strong religious beliefs, those same-sex desires were even more devastating because they were against the teaching of God's Word. What if people found out? What would they think? What would you, Mom or Dad, say or do? How would the rest of the family feel? This has been their *big secret* and tremendous burden for many years. And now you know.

So what about you, Mom and Dad? Has your child's secret now become your secret too? Are you afraid of what the rest of your family will think and how your community will react? Discovering your child's SSA is a difficult passage, but it can also mark the beginning of a new and wonderful journey. Once you begin to follow the steps offered in this book, you will be able to create the support network you need. You'll learn to reach out to God for love and renewal. And with his help, you will discover that it is possible to find hope and healing for your SSA child, for yourself and for your entire family.

Today there are more answers than ever to the questions surrounding same-sex attractions. And with those answers comes hope for restored love and even a change in sexual orientation. In spite of current cultural messages to the contrary, over eighty years of scientific research show that women and men who experience SSA are stuck in an early stage of psychosexual development because of hurts and deficits. If their wounds are addressed and if their unmet needs for love and attachment are fulfilled in healthy relationships, healing and change are possible.

As you will see, same-sex attraction is not really about sex at all. SSA has to do with a sense of not belonging, not fitting in, feeling on the outside, being somehow different. A boy feels "less than" and unlike the other guys; he may have been called "faggot," "queer," "sissy" or "gay" at school. A girl feels different too and doesn't think she belongs with other girls. She may have been called "dyke," "lesbian," "tomboy" or "gay." Same-sex attraction is about internalized emotions of detachment and is created over years of confusion and pain. It may take many more years to undo the damage that has been done.

Consider these wise words: "The process by which a homosexually inclined man or woman finally reaches the destiny of solid homosexual commitment is a very long one. By the time a person is ready for his 'coming out' (as the patois of the gay world has it), it might seem that the opportunity for preventive steps is past. But this is usually not so. Quite likely, the homosexual-to-be is in a state of great anxiety and indecision. Quite possibly, he is also casting about desperately for a source of help."[3]

Indoctrination into "Innate, Immutable" Mythology

While you are battling for your child's heart and soul, others have their own interest in his or her sexual orientation. In 1989, Marshall Kirk and Hunter Madsen published the homosexual manifesto titled *After the Ball: How America Will Conquer Its Fear and Hatred of Gays in the '90s*. Kirk, a researcher in neuropsychiatry, a logician, a poet and a Harvard graduate, together with Madsen, an expert in public persuasion tactics and social marketing with a Ph.D. from Harvard, designed a plan to homosexualize America and the world as defined in their book *After the Ball*.[4]

Since the publication of *After the Ball*, institutions of science, politics and religion, and the media and entertainment industries have been indoctrinated into the "innate, immutable" mythology: you are born gay and you cannot change. This was part of the strategic plan, a well-crafted Madison Avenue marketing extravaganza to normalize homosexuality as just another variation of human sexuality. This myth has no foundation in scientific research.[5]

As a result of the public-relations campaign to promote this theory of homosexuality, gender-confused children today have been persuaded

---

[3]Peter and Barbara Wyden, *Growing Up Straight: What Every Thoughtful Parent Should Know About Homosexuality* (New York: Stein and Day, 1968), p. 179.

[4]If you would like to read a summary of the book, e-mail me at info@gaytostraight.org, and I will be happy to send you a sixteen-page encapsulation of their theory and strategy. If you want to read the book: Marshall Kirk and Hunter Madsen, *After the Ball: How America Will Conquer Its Fear and Hatred of Gays in the '90s* (New York: Plume, 1989).

[5]For more facts about the false genetic and biological claims on the origins of homosexuality, please read *Homosexuality and the Politics of Truth* by Jeffrey Satinover, M.D.; *The Trojan Coach* by Jeffrey Satinover, M.D. (www.narth.com); and *My Genes Made Me Do It* by Dr. Neil and Briar Whitehead.

that they are genetically homosexual; they have been led to believe that being "gay" is who and what they are and that homosexuality is the essence of their being. Although same-sex attraction, in truth, is a manifestation of desire or behavior resulting from past wounds and unmet love needs, these young people have not learned to make a distinction in their minds between gay identity and homosexual behavior. The two concepts have become synonymous through films, news, magazine articles, music, video, novels, textbooks, Internet, radio interviews and every other media outlet imaginable. Kids who experience SSA believe, "I'm gay. It's who I am. My homosexual behavior is simply an extension of my core identity. I was born this way."

Meanwhile children who grow up in religious homes face an even greater battleground. Before their parents know anything about their inner conflict, most often they beg God to rid them of their homosexual feelings. They might have prayed day after day, month after month and year after year: "Please, God, take away these homosexual desires. I can't stand it anymore. I would rather die than have these feelings." But their prayers go unanswered. This doesn't happen because God wasn't listening, but because they, like me, prayed the wrong prayer. We should have prayed, "God, please reveal the true meaning of my homosexual desires. And then, Lord, please help bring healing to each one of those areas of my life."[6]

Stages of "Coming Out"

Because I have wrestled with homosexual desires and same-sex attraction myself, I can relate to the process your loved one has probably gone through. It may be helpful for you to read and think about the seven stages of development that usually precede the "coming out" declaration.

---

[6] I suggest that you not tell your child to start praying this way unless he is willing to change. Otherwise it may have a reverse and damaging effect, particularly if the child believes he was born homosexual.

Stage 1: Causes of SSA. There are many contributing factors that can result in homosexual desires. Some of the causes of SSA may be disrupted attachment between father and son or mother and daughter (this may strictly be the child's perception, not the parent's failure), overattachment to the opposite-sex parent, hypersensitivity, lack of bonding with same-sex peers, sibling wounds, cultural wounds, name-calling, sexual abuse and body image wounds. There is never one thing alone that causes SSA. A combination of several variables leads to homosexual desires in men or women. Please read other books for a more extensive understanding about the etiology of SSA.[7]

Stage 2: Same-sex attractions begin. SSA emerges at a different age for each person, depending on several factors: the child's temperament, physiology and perceptions; family history at particular times; and social or cultural events. You will have to check with your child to find out when she began to experience SSA. Be careful to distinguish between her envy of a person of the same gender and the sexualization of that envy. Those are separate and distinct issues. Most often, the eroticization of another person of the same gender begins at around ten to thirteen years of age, somewhere around the onset of puberty. But there are exceptions, and those desires may emerge later on, in the late teens or early twenties.

Stage 3: Conflict over SSA. The young struggler may ask himself, "Why do I have these feelings? What would others think of me if they knew I had homosexual desires?" A girl may wonder, "Is it a sin to feel this way? Does God still love me?" Most often, these boys and girls experience tremendous feelings of pain, confusion, guilt, shame, denial, loneliness and despair. These emotions are exacerbated when the young person is unable or unwilling to talk freely with family and friends.

---

[7]Richard Cohen, *Coming Out Straight;* Joseph Nicolosi, *Reparative Therapy of Male Homosexuality;* Alan Medinger, *Growth into Manhood;* Anne Paulk, *Restoring Sexual Identity: Hope for Women Who Struggle with Same-Sex Attraction.* For a more complete list, see "Recommended Reading List" at the back of this book.

Instead today's kids easily find "answers" outside their immediate circle of loved ones. They can access pro-homosexual information on the web or attend a Gay Straight Alliance (GSA) meeting in high school or a Gay Lesbian Bisexual Transgender (GLBT) meeting in college. The new addition to the GLBT nomenclature is "Questioning Youth," so that people who have a fleeting attraction for someone of the same gender may be led to believe that they too are "gay."

Stage 4: Need for belonging. The struggle continues: "I don't fit in. I don't belong. I'm not like the other kids." During puberty, what were once emotional desires for same-sex bonding now become sexually inflamed yearnings. The emotional need for nonsexual intimacy with the same-sex parent and/or same-sex peers suddenly becomes eroticized. However intense the desire may feel, it is important to remember that the basis for all SSA is conflicted emotional need, not sexual attraction. Same-sex attractions represent the following:

- An unconscious drive for bonding with the same-sex parent and/or same-sex peers because of homo-emotional and homo-social wounding.

- The need for gender identification. Since there was insufficient bonding with their same-sex parent and/or same-sex peers, they seek to join with members of the same gender in order to internalize their missing sense of masculinity or femininity.

- Fear of intimacy with members of the opposite sex. There may be overattachment between mother and son or father and daughter or an abusive relationship with a member of the opposite sex. Either will preclude healthy heterosexual desires.

Stage 5: Indoctrination. As we've seen, anyone who experiences the least amount of same-sex attraction is told, "You were born gay. You cannot change. Efforts to change are harmful." These youngsters have to work very hard to accept themselves as "gay" or "lesbian." The process generates conflicting thoughts and feelings. I believe that those who experience SSA initially know, in their heart of hearts, that homosexual behavior is out of sync with natural law. Nonetheless, they are inundated with the idea that it is a genetically determined condition, which amounts to a "mythology of homosexuality."

The "born gay" myth is much like the old tale *The Emperor's New Clothes*. In this folk tale, an emperor is fooled into thinking skilled craftsmen are creating beautiful clothes for him. In fact, two charlatans create nothing at all. Going along with the hoax, the emperor parades through the city streets wearing nothing. Not wanting to appear foolish, all his subjects exclaim, "What a wonderful set of new clothes!" Then a child stands up and says, "The emperor is naked!" At that moment the emperor realizes he has been duped. "We should all be like this child and speak the truth," he proclaims.

And so it is today. Innumerable people have been deceived, even though everyone knows that humans are heterosexually designed. In short, a man and a woman fit together perfectly and naturally. Two men or two women do not.

Stage 6: Identity acceptance as gay, lesbian, bisexual or transgender. At this juncture, strugglers come to terms with their SSA and adopt a "gay," "lesbian," "bisexual" or "transgender" identity. They have anesthetized their conscience through self-acceptance and social indoctrination. Hearing the homosexuality myth repeated often enough, with little or no debate, establishes it as fact. At this stage, you and the rest of the "homophobic" society may be perceived as the enemy.[8] "You don't understand. You don't know what it's like to be gay and be on the outside looking in." The us versus them complex is reinforced.

Stage 7: "Coming out" process. Often parents are the last to know

---

[8]A phobia is an irrational fear of something, not a principled disagreement. "Gay" activists have misused this term.

about a child's SSA. Gender-confused young people are especially sensitive and fearful of rejection, so they first "come out" to their friends or siblings. When they finally talk to you, their parents, they may say something like, "Please accept me for who I am. I'm your gay child. God made me this way!" Or they may angrily exclaim, "If you refuse to accept me just the way I am, you're incredibly homophobic and unloving." Above all else, they are afraid to lose your love after working through years of emotional, mental, physical and spiritual angst to come to terms with their SSA.

But what if you don't wish to accept or applaud your child's chosen way of life? What if you refuse to internalize the current sociopolitical definition of SSA? How do you and your child live with two conflicting paradigms? Here's the big question: Can you still love your child and yet completely disagree with his choice to adopt a "gay" identity?[9]

The short answer is, Yes, you can. In the pages that follow you will discover how to unconditionally love your child. You will gain understanding about the dynamics that led her into SSA and beyond, and perhaps into homosexual behavior. And you will find ways to create a strategic plan for bringing gifts of healing and loving attachment with your child.

Probably the most important thing to remember as you begin to reach out to your SSA child is that your love must be unconditional. If you give the impression either directly or indirectly that you hope, by loving your child more, that he will "change," leaving homosexuality behind, your best efforts will almost certainly be rejected. If you indi-

---

[9]There are two independent organizations for parents of "gays" now in existence. One is PFOX (Parents and Friends of Ex-Gays and Gays), which encourages parents to love their children while believing that no one is born with SSA and that change from homosexual to heterosexual is possible. (Some faith-based ministries, such as JONAH, Courage, Exodus and Evergreen, have separate support groups for family and friends. Their philosophy is similar to PFOX's.) The other is PFLAG (Parents and Friends of Lesbians and Gays), which encourages parents to embrace their children and accept their homosexuality as innate and immutable.

cate that bringing about change is your intention, your efforts will look like cynical manipulation to your child. Please keep in mind that love must be offered unconditionally. "Freely you have received, freely give."

Love cannot have a price tag attached that says, "I'll love you freely for now, but to keep my love forever, you'll have to give me something. You'll have to stop being the way you are." Not only is this a misguided approach, but you can be sure your child has already been warned against the concept of "change" by pro-gay ideologues. Before you even think about discussing the possibility of transitioning from a homosexual to a heterosexual orientation, be aware of the messages she has learned:

- This type of therapy leads to suicide and depression.
- It does not work and creates more harm than good.
- The possibility of change is rejected by the popular scientific and medical organizations.
- Those who practice and promote this type of therapy (pejoratively called "conversion therapy") are homophobic and anti-gay.
- Anyone believing in the change of sexual orientation is part of the "religious right" or is a hateful, anti-gay therapist.

These messages are scientifically unfounded and simply untrue.[10]

It may have taken your child years to accept his SSA as innate and immutable. If you were to say, "But you can change," his gut response would be, "No way. I have worked too hard to accept myself as gay. I don't want to go back and see if what you say is true." Put yourself in

---

[10]Dr. Robert Spitzer of Columbia University published a study in the *Archives of Sexual Behavior* (October 2003) clearly showing that people can and do change their sexual orientation. For an extensive list of research demonstrating the efficacy of change, please go to www.becomingreal.org/articles/articles.htm. Visit other websites to view stories of personal transformation from a homosexual to a heterosexual orientation (<www.peoplecanchange.com>; <www.jonahweb.org>; <www.pathinfo.org>).

your child's shoes. Would you, after wrestling to accept your SSA, want to deconstruct the whole situation? It is not an appealing proposition. And that is where you come in.

✖ Our strategy is to love these children as God loves us—flaws and confusion and mistaken identities and all. As we love them, we reawaken the lost, hurt child within. Then, with great care and gentleness, we seek to reattach that hurt child to the same-sex parent and same-sex peers. As you think about reaching out to your child, remember that a web of lies has been spun around him. Now, with love and truth, you must try to reverse the damage and restore your child.

✖ *Our solution to SSA is love and understanding. All same-sex attractions are based on two things: (1) childhood wounds that have not healed, and (2) unmet needs for love and acceptance. That's it. If you focus on those two things, you can help your child heal into the fullness of true gender identity and fulfill her heterosexual potential.*

It works if you work the program.

It's All About Belonging

Everyone needs to belong, whether to a family, community, religion, tribe or country. Many of those with SSA feel they've never fit in; they've never belonged anywhere. While keeping her painful secret from you, she faked "belonging" with you but never felt it in her heart. And now she thinks she does belong; she believes that she has found acceptance and compassion in the homosexual community.

I hope to assist you in helping your child and family heal. That healing is all about creating an authentic environment of belonging. The healing of SSA is about creating secure attachment. It is about bonding with the same-sex parent and same-sex peers in healthy, healing ways. We do not seek to do this to manipulate our SSA loved one. We do it because a wrong needs to be made right. We do it because deep wounds must be healed. And change ensues when healing occurs.

Most often an SSA son did not internalize his father's love, over-identified with his mother and the feminine, and felt abandoned or rejected by his same-sex peers. For these reasons, and perhaps others, he lacks a sense of his own gender identity.

The same holds true for the SSA daughter. She may have failed to bond sufficiently with mom and same-sex peers, she may have over-identified with Dad and his masculine ways, or she may have been abused by men. Somewhere along the way she did not internalize a healthy sense of her own femininity. If the parent-child attachment had been secure, she would not have SSA.

Please bear in mind that none of this is a comment or criticism about your parenting. It is all about perception. Generally these are very sensitive children. They easily get hurt and detach emotionally, often without your knowledge.[11] You, however, are in a position to make an enormous difference in your child's life today.

This Is a Battle of Love

As you prepare yourself for this new effort, you will need emotional, mental, physical and spiritual fortitude. Always remember that your child deeply fears losing your love. Although he may have been coached about how to "come out," he is still afraid that you will withdraw your love and attention. All his conversations with you will have a subtext: "Do you accept me as I am?" What your child is really saying is, "Do you still love me, or will you reject me?"

Many parents have asked me, "How long will this take, and what are the necessary steps to win my child back?" The length of time required will largely depend on four elements: (1) your tenacity, (2) your child's receptivity, (3) the severity of your child's wounding and (4) God's tim-

---

[11]Joseph Nicolosi, *Reparative Therapy of Male Homosexuality* (Northvale, N.J.: Jason Aronson, 1991), p. 34.

ing. As you will see in this treatment plan, there are many positive things for you to do. The more time you invest, the greater the results. Concerning the efforts necessary to win your child back, here is a brief overview of the process:

1. *Educate yourself about the causes of SSA.* Read books and articles, listen to audiotapes or CDs, watch videos or DVDs that talk about the causes and healing of homosexuality, and attend parental support groups such as PFOX, JONAH, Exodus, Courage or Evergreen International, which can help you understand the truth about homosexuality. Study sources from Positive Alternatives to Homosexuality (www.pathinfo.org) will help you understand how change of orientation happens. (For more information, see "Recommended Reading List" and "International Resources" at the back of this book.)

Some parents and loved ones will have to make the journey from disgust to compassion. It is natural to think about homosexual behavior as unpleasant. This is a visceral reaction to something we do not understand. That is why it is imperative to learn about the truth of same-sex attraction, to listen to individuals who have suffered with these feelings and finally to come to a place of deep compassion for their journey. This will take time.

2. *Educate yourself about the homosexual movement and what your child has learned.* To learn more about the information to which your child has been exposed, read pro-homosexual books, newspapers and magazines, attend PFLAG meetings and view pro-homosexual websites. (See a list of these websites in the back of this book.) It is important for you to understand how and why your child thinks about being "gay" or "lesbian." Therefore spend time learning about pro-gay philosophy. This will give you deeper insight into your child's worldview.

3. *Realize you are now entering your child's world.* You are feeling and experiencing what your son or daughter has already been going through, perhaps for years: confusion, hurt, denial, pain, anger, shock,

guilt, shame and betrayal. In short, the question you will continually ask yourself is, "Why me?" Ask for support from family, friends and your spiritual community, while bearing in mind that many will have accepted the gay affirmative agenda and thus may not be as helpful as you wish. Attend support groups for parents or participate in our teleconferencing classes via the telephone.[12] Take care of yourself. Take care of your relationship with your spouse (if you are married). Keep things in balance while seeking God's comfort and guidance.

4. Join with your child. Grieve with and for her. Listen, listen and listen. Be Mr. or Ms. KYMS (Keep Your Mouth Shut). Travel back in time with her to find out what she went through. This will demand much time, touch and talk. Be patient with yourself and your child. This process is more difficult if your child is not living at home, but I will make suggestions on how to work with kids who live elsewhere. And a word to the wise: expect rejection, but never give up.

5. Establish trust, do things together and attend meetings of their choice. Love, praise, stroke, hold, cherish and provide the unmet needs for love. This is particularly important for the same-sex parent to do. Use all the skills of the treatment plan in order to create secure attachment and a profound sense of belonging to *you*. Fathers, get more involved in your son's life. Mothers, do the same with your daughter. If she wants you to read one of their pro-homosexual books, magazines or articles, do so. If he wants you to attend a PFLAG meeting, go. It's important to demonstrate your love and care by "joining" in his world, seeing from their point of view. It does not mean that you condone the behavior or lifestyle. It

---

[12]The International Healing Foundation sponsors teleconferencing classes, a series of nine classes for parents conducted over a three-month period. Classes are held over the phone and last for one and a half hours. The first thirty minutes we teach about understanding homosexuality and how to help your child heal. The final sixty minutes is an open session of questions and answers. You receive personal coaching and gain the support of other parents in the class. (For more information, go to <www.ComingOutStraight.com> or call 301-805-6111.)

means that you love your child and want to understand her perspective.[13]

6. Seek professional help: therapy, seminars, family healing sessions.
Find local therapists who understand what you are trying to do and are
willing to assist. You may attend some of our healing seminars, participate
in private family healing sessions or attend other healing events for parent-
child attachment. If your son is interested in healing from unwanted SSA,
encourage him to attend a Journey Into Manhood (JIM) weekend, an Adventure in Manhood (AIM) weekend, or International Healing Foundation's Father-Son and Mother-Daughter Healing Seminars (see "Healing
Seminars and Family Healing Sessions" in the back of this book for more
information on these). You may also want to get involved in groups that
assist those with unwanted SSA. Do keep it in mind, however, not to push
too hard. If you do, you may trigger resistance or even rebellion.

As for your opinions, my advice is that you should state your beliefs
regarding homosexuality one time and one time only. Please do not repeat them over and over again. If you continue to hammer away on mor-
als and values, you will further distance your already-detached child and
lose valuable ground. You may think that if you don't constantly reiter-
ate, "I don't believe in homosexuality," your child will assume you are accepting his "gay" identity and go even deeper into that lifestyle. Your
constant negativity will only reinforce your child's sense of "not belonging" with you and will further distance her from a loving God. Nagging
about biblical law or God's displeasure will send SSA strugglers directly
into the arms of the sad gay world. Bear in mind that we flawed humans
need love the most when we deserve it the least.

An integral part of the SSA condition is *oppositional behavior*. As I have
seen again and again, those who experience homosexual desires are—

---

[13]Some parents have chosen to read their child's books and attend meetings if the child will do
likewise concerning the concept of change. While this strategy may work for some, it generally fails in the majority of cases. Do what they wish in order to get closer and create greater
intimacy.

consciously or unconsciously—deeply wounded. Unable to access their hurts, which often involves past family dynamics, they may do things to upset you as a means of retaliation. Above all else, they need your love, but perhaps they haven't experienced it to the degree they really need it. Please don't withhold your love or anything else, such as finances, in an effort to control your child's behavior. If the love you demonstrate toward your SSA child is conditional, withheld whenever you are displeased, you will widen the gap between you.

Therefore you may not experience a lot of love coming your way from your SSA child, at least not at first. Instead expect to be rejected when you make more efforts to love and listen. SSA men and women have many shields around their hearts, many defenses and many wounds that have been buried alive. Therefore initially they may reject your attempts at expressing love. Please hang in there. Don't let go, and eventually they will let you in.

In the beginning, you may find yourself doing the wrong thing and saying what appear to be the wrong words. Try not to worry or obsess about what you've said or done; mistakes happen to everyone because there is a huge learning curve. Simply ask your son or daughter to be patient with you, and while you try to find your way through the maze of challenges, extend grace both to your child and to yourself.

While you're at it, explain your efforts to your other children, relatives and friends. It is important to educate them about the truth of SSA and how they can help your child heal. Teach them about this strategic plan of love. Give them books to read, tapes/CDs to listen to and videos/DVDs to watch. Have them check out the websites designed to assist strugglers. And tactfully help correct the misinformation they might have picked up along the way.

Speak to your pastor, rabbi or priest. Some members of the clergy may have been deceived by gay affirmative propaganda on the one hand or may reject anyone who experiences same-sex attraction on the other.

Do your best to help your spiritual leaders understand what you have learned, and encourage them to walk with you through the process. If you find no openness to your plan, it might be wise to seek out another clergyman (or woman) who will support you in your efforts.

Three Types of SSA Children

In my experience, there are basically three types of SSA children. First, there are those who have unwanted SSA and wish to change; they want to come out straight. Second, there are those who are confused or undecided about their sexuality. They are not sure which direction to go in. And third, there are those who identify themselves as "gay," "lesbian," "bisexual" or "transgender." This last type believes the "innate, immutable" myth of homosexuality. They are convinced they were born this way and therefore change is not possible.

Of course, it is easier to work with the first type of child because they are motivated to change. You may utilize all the suggested tools in this book, and most likely, your child will be receptive to your love, attention and affection. There may be some resistance from your son or daughter because of the defensive detachment that created the same-sex attractions in the first place. However, there is still common ground for cooperation. And please be aware, as part of their healing journey your child may establish new boundaries, learning to separate and individuate from either the opposite-sex parent, or both parents. This will be a healthy developmental task for your child as he or she begins to define his or her own personhood, perhaps for the very first time. Eventually your child will open up once again. But this time it will be as a more whole and healthy individual. I have coached many parents whose children are invested in their own healing, and the process goes much faster when both parents and children are involved.

All the principles taught in this treatment plan apply to the second type of children, those who are confused or undecided about their sexuality. If your child is still living at home and you implement this plan as soon as possible, you may prevent him or her from going down the road that leads to a "gay" or "lesbian" identity. If your child is living on his or her own, there is still much you can do to help healing occur. Of course it is much more difficult, but definitely possible. Please read two wonderful stories of transformation at the end of steps eight and ten; these families helped their confused children come out straight.

And finally, the third type of children are those who believe they were born with SSA. All the same tools and principles of parenting apply to them as well. The only difference is, in most cases, it will take longer to break through. There are two reasons for this: (1) your child or loved one has a mental block—"I'm gay and that's that"—which prohibits them from exploring the root causes of their SSA, and (2) they have many defensive shields and guards around both their heart and mind which keep you at bay. This makes it a bit more challenging, but nonetheless possible, to help them eventually experience their true gender identity and come into the fullness of their innate heterosexuality.

The good news is that this program works with all types of SSA children. I have successfully coached parents who have children that desire change, children questioning their sexuality and children who identify as "gay" or "lesbian." Using these tools and skills on a regular and consistent basis has allowed them to break through with their SSA sons and daughters. You will read some of their wonderful stories of healing throughout the book.

Several keys to success are patience, consistency and a positive attitude. Practice using the helpful skills that you will learn in this plan. Keep a positive attitude, keep pouring the right kinds of love into your child, have others support this endeavor, and pray for God's continued intervention and guidance, and eventually there will be a change in the family system. *It is just a matter of time.*

You will need to take care of yourself while giving to your SSA child.

Healing is a journey, not a destination. You are now involved with setting love in order. If you continue to express healthy affection, affirmation and acceptance of your child (not accepting the "gay" or "lesbian" identity, but their true personhood), then eventually you will move into her or his heart and break it wide open. Again, it's just a matter of time.

Only God Can Do the Changing

Trust God to change your SSA child. As you do your work, you can be confident that God will be working as well. Use the treatment plan and tools to create greater intimacy. Once you successfully create an environ-ment of belonging, it will be the fertile and rich soil in which your child may heal and grow into his true gender identity.

The goal of this treatment plan is to create greater intimacy and secure attachment with your SSA child.

It is important to remind ourselves that it is not our responsibility to change any-one. It's hard enough to change ourselves! And who has been successful in changing a spouse over the course of marriage?

There are three basic ways to assist in the process of transformation:

1. Change yourself. As Gandhi said, "Be the change you wish to see in the world."

2. Provide an outpouring of love, in all its forms, by employing the strategies you find in this book.

3. Set an example with your steadfast and unconditional love, bearing in mind that most SSA relationships do not last.

I've heard some SSA kids say, "Oh, so now I'm your *project*." You might respond by saying, "Yes, you are my project of love. I will love you with all of my life, no matter what. Please teach me what you need. I will never let you go!" Come what may, put your faith in God and do your best. He will do the rest.

Never Give Up

SSA represents a person's detachment from his sense of being masculine or her sense of being feminine. If secure attachment can be established between your child and the same-sex parent as well as with gender-secure, same-sex role models, and healthy boundaries established with your child and the opposite-sex parent, he will then be on the right track toward potential healing of his gender identity. When a man feels his masculinity, he will be attracted to the opposite, a woman. When a woman feels her femininity, she will be attracted to the opposite, a man.

When SSA women and men work through their core wounds, their lives will be transformed in the process. And as you participate, your life will be transformed too. Both you and your son or daughter will experience more love and compassion. By opening your heart to your wounded child, you too will grow and be healed. Keep these four things in mind during the process:

1. Your child is wounded and needs secure attachment with the same-sex parent and same-sex peers.

2. The point is not being gay or straight; it is experiencing one's true gender identity.

3. SSA is a developmental issue and, essentially, not about sex.

4. SSA often has to do with unhealthy attachment to the opposite-sex parent or other members of the opposite sex.

Three Aspects of Healing

This book is divided into three sections. Section one is about *personal* healing: taking care of yourself, dealing with your own issues and experiencing God's love. Section two is about *relational* healing: understanding the causes of your loved one's SSA, learning effective communication skills, setting love in order, creating greater intimacy with your child, discovering her love language and displaying appropriate affection. Section three is about *community* healing: creating a welcoming environment in your home and place of worship, relating to your child's partner and finding mentors to assist in the healing process.

You may want to read the sections in the order they appear. However, for reasons of your own, you might wish instead to focus on a step that speaks to you in a particular moment. I do hope that, eventually, you will read the entire book and apply it to your circumstances. By assimilating these concepts and practicing these skills, you will begin to sense how to respond to your child in any given situation. Rereading the book will help you integrate these concepts into your daily life.

Take one step at a time and remember that you don't need to do too many activities at once. Most of all, understand that these are suggestions, a means to an end. As you find ways to display love to your SSA child, be patient with yourself. Always remember, *whoever loves the most and longest wins.* And, last but not least, keep in mind those three words that have given me strength through some of the greatest challenges of my life: *Never give up.*

Section One

PERSONAL HEALING

Section one is about taking care of yourself, dealing with your personal issues and experiencing God's love. You will encounter many emotions along the way. It is important to take care of yourself and your marriage (if you are married). If you want your child to heal, work on healing yourself. Lead by example. Seek support from your family, friends, spiritual community and God.

- Step One: Take Care of Yourself
- Step Two: Do Your Own Work
- Step Three: Experience God's Love

STEP ONE
Take Care of Yourself

Self-care is crucial when dealing with a loved one's SSA. You will need to handle your emotions, thoughts and spiritual life in healthy ways. Generally it is easier to talk about drug, alcohol or sexual addictions with others than it is to discuss the issue of homosexuality. We have come a long way in dealing with these other issues, but there is still additional shame when dealing with SSA—for your child and also for you. We can change this discrepancy only through education. Educate yourself first, then your loved ones and finally the supportive community around you.

Initial feelings and emotions that you may continue to experience may include shock, denial, guilt, shame, disgust, confusion, loss, anger, sadness, betrayal, mistrust, numbness, fear and grief. You will probably say it a thousand times: "I can't believe this is happening to me!" Yes, it is devastating. Few parents would want their child to have to deal with homosexuality. Life is rough enough. But here it is, and it is no longer about "them." It's about you and your child.

Be Gracious to Yourself

Be gracious to yourself. Feelings are feelings. They are neither good nor bad; they just are. And you will go through many of them over and over again. You may experience feelings of repulsion or recoil, or as one parent called it in teleconferencing class, the "yuck" factor. This is a gut response to homosexuality that most people experience. It is a built-in biological defense to what we do not understand or what we fear. For anyone who has never experienced SSA, the gut reaction is usually, "Yuck! How could anyone want such a thing? It's against nature." Yes, it is against natural law. However, your child has wrestled with SSA for many reasons and has fought long and hard to gain self-acceptance. By now homosexual desires feel natural to her.

Authors Peter and Barbara Wyden explain:

> [One] reason why so many people shy away from our subject is the common conviction that homosexuality is incurable. This was long believed to be true about cancer, and it made cancer an unspeakable subject. But in recent years, news about the curability of cancer has spread considerably, and the topic is no longer taboo. News about the curability of homosexuality has not spread. A more significant difference is that while many forms of cancer are not readily preventable, most homosexuality—conceivably almost all—probably is.[1]

Another area that might cause you to recoil has to do with our ideas about the traditional family. The homosexual community is redefining the family through same-sex couples, adoption and bearing children through artificial insemination. In all likelihood, this is not what you dreamed of or wished for your child's future. The revelation of her homosexuality might well involve the loss of your dreams for her marriage and your grandchildren.

What you will come to realize through this journey is that you must resist your gut reactions—your defensive physiology—and focus instead on the causes and healing of SSA. That is the best way for you to respond to your child and others with SSA—displaying the right kind of love that is deeper than mere emotion. Much of what you will need to say and do will be counterintuitive to the yuck factor. This process will take time,

---

[1]Peter and Barbara Wyden, *Growing Up Straight* (New York: Stein and Day, 1968), p. 18.

so be patient with yourself and your loved ones. Ask them to be patient with you. You are, after all, in a process that is very similar to that of grieving a significant loss.

Recognize the Five Stages of Grieving

Dr. Elisabeth Kübler-Ross speaks of five stages of grieving in her classic book *On Death and Dying*.[2] Here are the basic steps, each of which is applicable to finding out that your child has SSA:

1. Denial: "This can't be happening to me/us/him/her."

2. Anger: "Why did this happen? I did my best."

3. Bargaining: "Please God, if we do _____, change him/her."

4. Depression: "It's true, and I can't stand this. It's too painful. I want my child to marry and have children. My dreams are lost."

5. Acceptance: "Okay, this is true. What now? What can I do to assist him/her? How can I take care of myself in the process?"

You will revisit these stages over and over again. It is important to keep expressing your feelings and thoughts to your spouse, friends and loved ones as well as to yourself and God. The more you are able to express yourself, the more quickly you will pass through the five stages. As the saying goes, "You must feel and be real in order to heal." Feelings that are buried alive never really die. If left unexpressed, they get repressed, which further complicates the situation.

Do not try to manage things on your own. We exist in relationships. If you share your thoughts and feelings only with God or your pillow at night, you are prolonging the process of healing. This will not serve you or your child. Find others with whom to share your feelings.

While you are dealing with your child's SSA, you may find yourself

---

[2]Elisabeth Kübler-Ross, M.D., *On Death and Dying* (New York: Collier, 1969).

burdened with guilt. "It's all my fault" is a natural reaction, but it simply isn't true. You can be sure that there are many potential causes for your child's SSA. An important point to realize and remember is this: It is not the parenting that creates SSA in men or women. It is the child's temperament combined with his perception of the parenting and other social influences that makes all the difference. Perception becomes reality.

Most children who develop SSA are highly sensitive and easily hurt. After experiencing some hurt, they easily cut off and detach emotionally—with or without your awareness. That is when the relationship gets derailed. The healing of SSA is about retracing those steps, getting back to where things went off track and reconnecting in a healthy way with oneself and one's parents.

Yes, you will experience many difficult emotions. Be assured that there is no "right" way to go through this. Take your time. Share your heart with God and others. One parent in a teleconferencing class commented, "Why did God do this to me and our son? I am so angry and confused. I am overwhelmed and cannot cope with this!" She was hurt and upset for many months. But finally, after studying and listening to the teachings and experiences of other parents, her final comment was, "I've learned that God did not do this to my son. I felt betrayed by him . . . but I finally came to the realization that he did not make this happen."

The process of grieving takes time and has its own rhythm.[3]

SSA Isn't Really About Sex

As we've seen, SSA springs from many sources. Primarily it relates to unhealed emotional wounds and needs for love that remained unmet. Your work will be easier if you focus on your child's wounded heart, not on sexual behavior. Seek the hurt child within the adolescent or adult, a

---

[3]Granger E. Westberg, *Good Grief*, 35th ed. (Minneapolis: Fortress Press, 1997). Westberg describes the many stages of grief, which have a direct relationship to your own experiences with your SSA child.

child who is crying out for love. <u>You are the answer, not</u> <u>not her girlfriend. You are the solution to healing your l</u> which is the story of a wounded child searching for love in an ... places and in all the wrong ways.

Welcome to Your Child's World

After finding out about a child's SSA, you probably went through the stages of shock, pain, grief, denial, confusion, hopelessness and "Why me?" This is the same process your child has probably gone through for years, though you never knew it. "Welcome to my world," your son or daughter might be saying to you. Isn't that painful to think about?

Without their parents' knowledge, SSA youngsters are forced to deal with this "unwanted harvest." <u>It took them many years and tears to come to a place of acceptance. You are now entering their world. It is painful. It is unknown. Share your thoughts and feelings with your child. Grieve together if you are comfortable in doing so. See the situation from his point of view; your child has so much to teach you.</u>

After discussing this idea in a teleconferencing class one evening, a mother sent me a lengthy e-mail. Every word rings true:

Your comment, "Welcome to Peter's world," was a turning point in our healing journey. In mid-April I was feeling very overwhelmed with my efforts to deal with Peter's SSA. He was approaching his twenty-sixth birthday, and as I reminisced over the years, I had intense feelings of being a failure as his mother. It had been ten months since I found out about Peter's SSA. I was overwhelmed with feelings of disbelief and guilt, and a painful sadness that tore at my heart every waking moment. Fear of the unknown with the scope of what we were faced with regarding his SSA haunted me. Frightened, oh so frightened, for what lay ahead for him and us in this SSA lifestyle . . . isolation, loneliness, AIDS, rejection of family and society, and a host of things I could only imagine. I was embarrassed, ashamed, scared and very, very sad.

It was at this time during our Parent's Teleconferencing Class when I was sharing these feelings that you very simply stated, "Welcome to Peter's world!" In that instant I knew for the very first time that I was experiencing just a microcosm of what day-to-day life was like for Peter. I was humbled. When he had shared his feelings and his SSA journey with us, it was just that, his journey. Even though we had talked with him, cried with him, and he shared the same feeling words with us about his experience, we had not fully related. In that simple statement, "Welcome to Peter's world," we had unity of feelings with our son. We had a newfound respect for what it must have been like for him during the time he dealt with his SSA on his own, searching for answers, praying, reaching out in all the wrong places.

With our newfound perspective, Harry and I forged a new relationship with Peter. There is a new respect between us. For the very first time we are, in some ways, walking in his shoes. We are different. Once we changed our perspectives, we began to notice a change in Peter. He has a new attitude toward us, a more genuine sensitivity. We talked with him, cried with him and told him, for the first time, we realized our feelings very closely reflected his. We had no idea of the magnitude of what he was and is dealing with until we tried to deal with it ourselves.

Peter's world is not an easy one. But it is the one in which he lives. We are blessed to have been given genuine insight into his world no matter how frightening it is, for him and for us. Now the journey is under way to help him make his world the best possible place it can be. With God's grace and Richard's guidance, hope is the new feeling we share with Peter.

Acknowledge Name-Calling and Rejection

Imagine going to school each day and wondering when the next kid will say to you, "Hey, faggot, get the hell out of here!" or "You dyke! Go play with the boys!" How would you feel? Such abuse hardly creates a wonderful and welcoming place to study and find friends. Yet your child might have experienced this at school.

How about going to the lunchroom and knowing that no one wants you to sit at their table? Or knowing in gym class that you will be the last one picked for the team? How would that make you feel? These are just some of the experiences your child may have lived through, in all likelihood without your knowledge. Many were mocked from the time they were in elementary school. It is very hurtful for any child to be called names. Those with SSA are prone to be hypersensitive; they are usually neither aggressive nor outspoken in their personalities. Chances are, you never heard about what happened to them at school when other kids ridiculed them.

Often kids use "gay" or "faggot" without actually meaning that the target of their abuse is someone dealing with SSA. They are simply using these words as general put-downs. However, if there is some homo-emotional or homo-social wounding already present in that child's heart, she begins to internalize these negative comments and may more easily accept the verdict "I'm gay."[4]

Imagine being in the church youth group where kids are joking about "the faggots," saying, "We should haul their asses out of town." One teenager I counseled said those were the exact comments of peers in his youth group. How do you think he felt? All this may be new to you, but most likely it is commonplace to your SSA child. You will need to listen and catch up with what your child has experienced.

---

[4]I use the term "homo-emotional wound" to describe a disrupted attachment between the child and same-gender parent. I use the term "homo-social wound" to denote a lack of bonding with same-gender peers.

Stop Self-Accusation

Initially you may blame yourself and/or your spouse for your child's SSA. Don't waste another minute: stop the blame game, because it does not help you, your spouse or your child. The only thing that will change the situation is taking personal responsibility for past mistakes, which means apologizing, making amends and creating a loving attachment between you, your spouse and your child. The rest of the treatment plan is all about taking these necessary steps into healing and reconciliation.

If you feel in need of it, receive God's forgiveness for whatever you may regret, and then forgive yourself. What you *can* do now is love God, love yourself and love others. Listen to your heart, be attentive and take care of your own needs in healthy ways. If you love yourself as God loves you, you will be better equipped to love your spouse and child.

Acute guilt is healthy. Chronic guilt is toxic. Here is an exercise to help relieve you of your guilt. Follow it step by step, and repeat as necessary. Use it with your spouse or a close friend, not with your SSA child. (I will discuss in step six how to apologize to your child directly.)

1. Write a list of things you feel bad about (things you said or did and things you didn't do that you wish you had done), for example, "As your mother, I kept you too close to me and said bad things about your father"; "As your father, I didn't spend enough time with you because I worked too much and I didn't understand your needs."

2. Role-play with your spouse or close friend. Have him play the part of your SSA child. Hold hands, imagining that you are sharing with your child. Read through your list. Look at the first sentence, and if it helps, close your eyes and imagine saying it directly to your child, apologizing for your inappropriate behavior or words. Breathe, express your feelings and then move

to the next sentence. Work through your list in this manner. Take your time. Grieve as necessary. Remember, we must feel in order to heal.

3. Allow your spouse or friend to respond as he believes your SSA child would (for example, offering forgiveness, rebuffing your apology or getting upset). Just listen. You don't need to respond unless you desire to do so.

4. After listening to the one role-playing your SSA child, close your eyes and ask God to forgive you for all these things. Then listen for his response. Be quiet. Wait on the Lord. Move to the next step after you receive an answer.

5. Finally, ask yourself for forgiveness. This may be the most difficult step to accomplish. It's easier to forgive others than it is to forgive ourselves. After receiving God's forgiveness, allow your spouse or trusted friend to play the role of you. Hold the person's hands and say, "[Your name], would you please forgive me for all these things?" Then close your eyes and listen to the voice within. There may be a lot of discourse and self-accusation. Just listen and let it all pour out. Don't censor, don't try to change the messages, just be a good listener. Again, you may have to ask the question, "[Your name], would you please forgive me for all these things?" Keep repeating the question, and keep listening until all the dialogue is complete and until the voice within says, "Yes, I forgive you."

You may need to repeat this exercise many times. Forgiveness in one's mind and forgiveness in one's heart take time. Again, ask your spouse or close friend to do this exercise with you. The sooner you receive God's forgiveness, and forgive yourself, the sooner you will be ready to take the necessary steps to help your child heal and grow.

Create an Alliance of Love

An "alliance of love" is what your family is about to become. This loving
alliance is essential between same-sex family members: father and son,
mother and daughter, brother and brother, sister and sister, grandfather
and grandson, grandmother and granddaughter, uncle and nephew,
aunt and niece. This is a suggestion that bears repeating, and you will
hear me say it again and again: *The goal of this twelve-step plan is to create
greater intimacy and secure attachment with your SSA child.* Change is a
byproduct of healing.

Dad, you may need to stretch your heart to understand your son.
Mom, you may need to stretch your heart to understand your daughter.
I have seen a double blessing occur in this process of reconciliation. By
consciously creating an alliance of love, you will bring your child closer,
you will experience more of your own humanity, and you will face your
shortcomings. As you seek healing for your child, you may find healing
for yourself in the process.

Grieve with Others

You cannot change the past. And it is unhealthy for you to live the rest
of your life in the shadow of self-blame. However, it is important to
grieve about what has happened. Grieve with others—your spouse, your
child, someone who cares and understands. Do not grieve alone; otherwise it will become cyclical and perhaps even obsessive. What was born
in broken relationships must be healed in healthy relationships. Consider joining a support group for parents sponsored by PFOX, JONAH
or another ministry. We grow and heal in relationships. If you want your
child to heal, lead by example. Heal yourself.

Create a Support System

As you seek support from family members, friends, religious leaders and your spiritual community, shame and guilt may try to stop you. If anyone judges you or your SSA child, please know that this kind of judgment isn't really about you or your child; it is about others and their lack of understanding SSA. What they and most people require is education about the truth of same-sex attraction and how they can be of assistance. (I talk more about this in section three of this book: "Community Healing.")

Create a supportive community around yourself, your spouse (if you have one) and your SSA child. Your support system may consist of, but not be limited to, the following:

- family members
- relatives, especially same-sex elders and peers
- close friends
- a spiritual leader
- friends from your place of worship
- members of support groups

Please don't try to carry this burden alone. It is important to surround yourself and your SSA child with a group of loving and caring men and women. This is a battle of love versus lies. Reach out and garner as much support as you possibly can.

Almost every SSA family member has said words like these:

I am afraid of telling other family members and friends about our child's homosexuality. I am afraid that when they find out, their opinion of our son and our family will change. Then the concept that our child is gay will be fixed in their minds, and the possibility of his coming out of homosexuality will become less and less.

I know you may have many fears, and some of them are based in unfortunate realities. I know that some people may have negative reactions when hearing about your child's SSA. Please allow me to reassure you that their reactions have nothing to do with you or your child and have everything to do with their ignorance about SSA. If someone says that homosexuality is a choice and your child must repent of this "sin," you need to educate that person about the truth of SSA: no one chooses to have homosexual desires; the choice is whether to act on those desires or not. (See step four for more details about the causes of SSA.)

The longer you resist opening up to others, the more you are blocking the opportunities for your child to grow. It takes a community to raise and heal a child. You too need support. If my parents had asked my brother, uncles, grandfathers and friends of the family to express love to me as much and as often as possible, I truly believe they would have saved me years of heartaches and pain.

Attend and Participate in Support Groups

You may want to look for local Parents and Friends of Ex-Gays and Gays (PFOX) or Jews Offering New Alternatives to Homosexuality (JONAH) chapters in your area. PFOX and JONAH have support groups throughout the country and world, and they offer online support groups. Several other organizations that offer assistance to men and women with unwanted SSA have parents groups as well: Exodus International (Christian), Evergreen International (Mormon), Courage/Encourage (Catholic), One by One (Presbyterian), Transforming Congregations (Methodist), Powerful Change Ministry Group (Christian/African American). PeopleCanChange.com offers online support groups for wives of men dealing with SSA. (Search the Positive Alternatives To Homosexuality [PATH] website, <www.pathinfo.org>, or see "International Resources" at the back of this book for more information on these and other groups.)

If you cannot find local assistance, the International Healing Foundation offers teleconferencing classes for parents. Through a series of nine

classes held over three months, we coach families in the process of reconciliation and in dealing with their SSA children. These classes also
provide a support group for parents (many call and e-mail each other
during the week).

It has been said, "When the child 'comes out,' the parents go in the
closet." We must destigmatize SSA for everyone's sake. Everywhere I go, I
share about the truth of SSA: at the post office, at my kids' schools, on the
soccer field watching my son's game. Today people are not as judgmental
and are more open to discussing homosexuality. Do not let that little voice
in your head that says, "What will people think?" stop you from sharing
and reaching out for help. We must educate everyone about the truth of
SSA so our kids have a chance to heal within their own community.

It is important to listen carefully to other parents who have SSA children. Learn from their mistakes and victories. You do not need to rein-
vent the wheel, and you do not have to be alone in your pain. Please do
not isolate yourself. By sharing with others who have SSA children, you
can gain strength in working toward a common goal. Join together and
inspire each other to continue on the path of healing. Pray together and
for one another. Extend your alliance of love to include these other parents. There is strength in numbers and power from mutual support.

Maintain Balance in Your Life

Do your best not to make your child's SSA the sole focus of your life. I
know for a fact that it's possible to become totally absorbed with this issue. I suggest that you make these your priorities:

1. Experience God's personal love.

2. Take care of yourself, maintain balance in your life, go out and
   have some fun. There is life apart from your child's SSA.

3. Take care of your marriage (if you are married).

Love yourself and love your spouse, and you will have more love to offer your children, especially your child with SSA. This process of bonding with your SSA child is going to require a lot of energy. Your love tank needs to be continuously refilled. Stop living in a state of worry, anger, guilt and fear. Instead be filled with joy and love. Find peace in the moment.

Do not get sucked into the SSA vacuum, feeling hopeless, helpless, discouraged and consumed with worry, guilt and shame. There may be a tendency to be obsessed with thoughts such as, *What if ____ finds out? What if she says, "You must have been a lousy parent. Why else would you have a child who is gay?"* You will need to choose carefully those with whom you share about your child's SSA, because there is so much judgment and rejection by those who should be the most loving and understanding. Sadly this is especially true in the religious community.

You may become exhausted and fed up from time to time, so this bears repeating: take time out for yourself, smell the roses, kick up your heels, play some games, have some fun, feed your soul, nourish the relationship with your spouse and spend time with friends.

This Is a Marathon, Not a Sprint

One father who successfully helped his son change from a homosexual to a heterosexual orientation began to limit his work time. Instead of putting in a sixty-hour workweek, he took off fifteen hours and began to devote that extra time to studying about SSA and to loving his son.

This wise father also renewed his spiritual life and garnered support from family and friends. He knew this path of healing would take time, so he created more time for his son. Within three years, his labor of love bore fruit. Instead of attending the GSA alliance at school, his son is now dating a young woman and hanging out with other guys (read his story at the end of step ten). But it didn't happen overnight. Remember, this is a marathon, not a sprint.

STEP TWO
Do Your Own Work

It may be tempting to blame your spouse or other people for your child's same-sex attraction. But please keep in mind that healing your relationship with your child is *not* a blame game. Although it is important to identify what may have taken place in the past, and it is essential to take positive steps toward reconciliation and restoration for the future, accusing others of being at fault in the situation is counterproductive. It is best for both parents to share the healing process together, to grieve together and to pray together. If spouses blame one another for past events, they create further distance between themselves, which invariably ends up being counterproductive in their efforts to restore their SSA child. Later we'll look at healthy ways to express thoughts and feelings without assigning blame (see step five).

Stop Pushing Your Spouse to "Do the Right Thing"

Without pointing fingers at one another, each parent will probably find it necessary to make certain changes in behavior and attitude toward the SSA child. No matter how necessary those changes may seem, do not nag, push, coerce or threaten your spouse regarding them. When you do so, you become your spouse's parent (wife becomes like her husband's mother, and husband would be like his wife's father)—and this creates an additional strain on the relationship. Your spouse will resent you, and your child will be the biggest loser of all.

Moms who have sons dealing with SSA and dads who have SSA

daughters, now is the time for you to take a backseat. Be a quiet encourager. Pray for bonding between father and son or mother and daughter. Shed tears with your spouse; express your pain about the situation. It is far better for us to show our feelings than to give orders. And we should grieve over our own mistakes, not our spouse's.

If the same-sex parent in your situation is unable to bond with the SSA child, then try—again, without accusing anyone—to find others to help. Take positive steps for your own well-being and that of your child. There are others in the community who may be better equipped to help your child experience healthy same-sex paternal or maternal love. Work with them to create secure attachment for your struggling daughter or son (see step twelve).

If You Want Your Child to Change, Change Yourself

As Peter and Barbara Wyden write,

> Before you embark on steps to redirect your child, you must face the possibility—indeed the strong likelihood—that changes will have to be made not only within your son or daughter but also within yourself, your spouse or both of you. . . . It is by no means necessary to be a "bad" or neglectful parent to be a homosexuality-inducing parent. Parents almost never encourage these tendencies with evil intent. Quite the contrary, many parental actions that encourage homosexuality actually stem from a mother or father's intense desire to do what they conceive to be their very best for the child's welfare.[1]

Your healing, both as an individual and as a couple, will have a positive impact on your SSA child as well as on the rest of your family. In the same way, unresolved issues will negatively influence your children. If

---

[1]Peter and Barbara Wyden, *Growing Up Straight* (New York: Stein and Day, 1968), pp. 23-24.

you truly want your son or daughter to heal, you will need to face your own fear, anger, sadness and disappointment. In doing so, you lead your child by example.

If you are hurting, grieve. If you are angry, express your feelings in a positive and assertive manner without hurting anybody else. Medicating your feelings through increased activities, blaming or using alcohol or drugs will serve only to delay progress—both yours and your child's. Instead I encourage you to face your feelings, trace their origins, release the pain, receive comfort from those you trust and create an action plan for personal, marital and family healing. It is essential to keep in mind—and you'll hear me say this again and again—that SSA is primarily a symptom of unhealed emotional wounds and unmet needs for love.

When a child falls down and scrapes his knee, he cries because it hurts. He does not need to hear promises that the pain will subside in a given amount of time or warnings that it is therefore unnecessary for him to cry. Nor does he need to be told about the nature of his cut and that the bleeding will stop once a scab forms. He simply needs you to hold him in your arms and listen to his pain.

"Mommy, Daddy, it *really hurts*," he cries.

"Yes, Son, we know it does, and we are here for you."

Once he hears those reassuring words, he begins to breathe more freely. Your loving touch and your caring presence start to heal his hurt and heart. Then you clean the scrape, apply some ointment and put on a Band-aid to protect the wound. Afterward he smiles, gives you a big kiss and says, "Thank you." And he is off to play once again.

That is how inner healing works too. The problem, however, is that most of us are afraid to express our hurt feelings; in fact, we may work very hard to keep them at bay. Worse than that, we may not even be in touch with our emotions. Yet we must feel in order to heal, and the more we demonstrate our willingness to be authentic, the more likely our children will be able to open up and share their hearts with us. Of course I am not saying that we should "dump" our issues on our children. We simply need to do our own work of inner healing, independently of them.

You probably felt powerless when you first had to face your child's SSA, because you could not control her behavior and thought process. If you tried, you quickly discovered that it only created a power struggle and caused more problems. Later I will offer many positive activities to promote relational intimacy. However, please be mindful that you cannot change your child. You can change only yourself. Please accept your limitations, and accept her right to be independent. Only then will you be able to create wonderful opportunities for healing and reconciliation.

To do this, you need to disentangle yourself from your child's SSA and/or homosexual behavior. Just as you should not blame others, you need to avoid blaming yourself. Self-blame may cause you to overreact and thus to become even more overinvolved. That, in turn, can prevent you from making necessary changes in your own life and marriage. Here are three unmistakable signs of being overly involved in your child's life:

1. Your child's SSA determines how you feel on a minute-by-minute, day-by-day basis.

2. Your preoccupation with your child's SSA causes you to neglect other people and activities in your life.

3. You act like a detective, trying to find out about your child's every move, looking and listening for clues much of the time.

In Search of Inner Health

One of the first tools I give to most of my clients is a workbook titled *Ten Days to Self-Esteem* by Dr. David Burns. It is a very simple and effective approach to dealing with negative thought processes and creating positive, rational responses. Dad and Mom, why not go through this workbook yourselves? I recommend doing one step every two weeks and regularly. In fact, you may want to consider doing the exercises at the same time and sharing your homework with your child. I counseled a father and his teenage son; both did the exercises, and it helped the dad as much as it encouraged his son.

Next I have my clients do "inner child" work by using Dr. Lucia Capacchione's *Recovery of Your Inner Child*, along with an inner-child meditation CD I have created. ("Inner child" is another name for our unconscious self, that which remains hidden from our conscious mind.) Using these two tools helps begin the process of getting in touch with feelings and needs. This is an essential part of the healing process, reawakening the precious little boy or girl we used to be.

It is important that we become good parents to ourselves, rather than expecting others to always take care of our needs. I also try to encourage my clients to get in touch with their feelings by using a very simple technique called focusing (see the book by that name by Eugene Gendlin). Through a six-step method, focusing helps us identify where in the body we feel our emotions, what the feeling is, where it comes from and what we need to do in response to it. This requires a lot of practice, but it is well worth the time. Through inner-child work and focusing, we gain a greater sense of self-worth and self-awareness.

Simultaneously it is essential to build a community of family and friends to surround and support you. Just as the SSA person needs others to aid in their healing, so do parents. We require a support system to strengthen and comfort us. Dads, find and connect with male friends who stand with you. Moms, make sure you have a number of trustworthy female friends. Whatever you do, avoid isolation from others. Going it alone will eventually prove to be counterproductive.

Do you want your child to open up and share hurts from the past? Again, "Be the change you wish to see in the world," as Gandhi said. Get help and support to resolve any outstanding issues you may have with your own parents, whether they are alive or deceased. It is never too late to heal. As you demonstrate your willingness to make peace with your parents, your children will feel more comfortable about opening up to you.

When you are doing your own work or therapy, you may choose to invite your children to participate in counseling sessions. It is a good way to enroll them into the healing process as this is a family affair. Use these magic words when inviting them into the session: "Would you please do it to help me?" Let them know it is about you and your issues, that you want them to participate so you can take responsibility for things that happened in the past. If you make the process about you, your child will feel less threatened and more inclined to attend. And do not single out the SSA child; make sure the entire family is included. Assuming there are siblings, invite all your children to be present. (See information about family healing sessions at the end of step six and addendum at the back of the book.)

Your child may be carrying some of your unhealed wounds and unmet love needs, or those of the family lineage (please see Exodus 34:6-7). Generally this amounts to a systemic repetition of lineage detachment between fathers and sons or mothers and daughters. Or it may represent intense wounding between those of the opposite sex: husbands and wives, mothers and sons, or fathers and daughters. These kinds of unresolved family issues can be internalized and manifest in your SSA child. The more actively you pursue your own healing and begin to treat your spouse and children in a more loving manner, the sooner the groundwork is laid for your SSA child's transformation.

Seek Couples Therapy

The best gift you can give your children is to love your spouse. We represent Mr. and Mrs. God to our kids, and disharmony in our marriages affects them deeply and directly. Meanwhile, dealing with a child's SSA—

always a stressful and delicate situation—will exacerbate any marital difficulties already present. With this in mind, consider finding a therapist who specializes in couples counseling. Take time to communicate and to work on your relationship, so you will both be stronger and more united. In short, if you are married, work hard on your marriage.

If there are no organizations or support groups in your area to suggest local referrals, contact the National Association for Research and Therapy of Homosexuality (NARTH) for a list of therapists throughout the country who believe in the possibility of change. However, even though NARTH therapists are supportive, they may have limited experience working with SSA families (see step four for the list of questions to ask prospective therapists). JONAH and Evergreen International also maintain a list of effective and skilled therapists who specialize in SSA issues, therapists of all religions and secular therapists as well. (See "International Resources" at the back of this book for more information on organizations.)

Be careful about contacting just any therapist. Most counselors today are educated and trained in "gay affirmative therapy." They have learned to encourage their clients to embrace SSA as "innate and immutable," and they will coach you, the parents, to accept your child's homosexuality. If you resist, they will tell you, "You are the problem, not your child." If you cannot find anyone in your area who is willing to work with you as you seek help for your child, contact Positive Alternatives to Homosexuality (PATH) organizations for further assistance.

Find Joy in Your Relationship

In the midst of all this, bear in mind that it is very important to balance your efforts with a measure of joy. It bears repeating that the best gift we can give our children is our love for one another. When they see restored unity and affection between dad and mom, they will feel more secure and at peace.

With this knowledge, be sure to add romance and spice to your life with your spouse. Go on dates together. Have fun. Do things that you both enjoy. Staying home and suffering serves no one, while the more love you generate between the two of you, the more love you will have for your children. So laugh. Watch funny movies. Stay away from issues and situations that will bring you down. Also, do not continuously subject yourselves to the subject of homosexuality. Instead make it your business to achieve balance, balance and more balance.

STEP THREE
Experience God's Love

If you believe in God and have a prayerful relationship with him, there may be a tendency for you to ask him for a proverbial silver bullet: "Dear Lord, please take away my child's SSA." Unfortunately things don't work that way. Allow me to suggest some more effective prayers.

- "God, please reveal to us the reasons our child experiences same-sex attractions."
- "God, why has this issue come into our family? For what greater purpose?"
- "God, please give me the strength and love to make it through today."
- "God, please show me how I can help my child heal. Reveal to me ways I can best love him/her."

For years, my own prayer was, "God, please take away these desires." When he didn't, I blamed him for my suffering. However, it was never my heavenly Father who gave me same-sex attractions. They were the result of a constellation of man-made factors: hypersensitive temperament, distant relationship with my father, sexual abuse from my uncle, antagonistic relationship with my older brother and overattachment to my mother. As each issue was revealed, God enabled me to heal them one by one. Today I am a much better man for it. So remember, I prayed the wrong prayer for over twenty-five years. I never received an answer because I was asking the wrong question. God could have removed my SSA in an instant, but that would not have healed my heart and soul.

Seek God's Help for Understanding and Direction

Instead of asking God to put a stop to the SSA right here, right now, pray for him to reveal to you and to your child the wounds that hide behind the SSA. Ask him for the strength, love and wisdom you need to help your child heal. Because this is a family affair, you may all grow and heal together. What was born out of broken relationships can and must be healed in healthy relationships.

If you truly desire to support your child's healing process, it is important for you to experience love and comfort from God. You cannot give what you do not experience. If you don't feel loved yourself, you won't be able to genuinely love anyone else. I encourage you to take all your confusion and painful feelings and hand them over to God. Fight, scream, cry and beg for mercy and understanding. You must seek him and his guidance with all your heart, with all your soul and with all your might. Don't stop until you have received the love, wisdom and direction you need.

You are not being punished. Your child's homosexuality is not some sort of retribution for errors that you or your spouse made. Although it may feel that way at times, this battle is not some sort of a curse or a stroke of bad luck or an omen of disaster. Ultimately you will find the good in the bad. It is through pain that we come to grips with our own humanity and weaknesses.

Sometimes difficult things happen so that the glory of God may be revealed in and through us. This may be one of those times in your life. I encourage you to rise to the occasion and to realize that you are not meant to handle this on your own. Read through the psalms. King David's anguish, pain, rage and surrender are evident throughout. Join with him and the other psalmists in calling out to the Lord. God will be close to your heart. He will not fail to hear and answer your petitions.

Pray Specific Prayers for Your Child

If you aren't sure how to pray for your child, consider some prayers and adapt them to your own circumstances with your son or daughter:

✓ • "God, please allow my daughter/son to experience Your love."

✓ • "Allow her/him to experience the fullness of her/his own femininity/masculinity."

✓ • "Please, dear God, bring healthy people into her/his life, those who might lead her/him into healing and the fulfillment of her/his true gender identity."

- • "Bless her/him with many healthy women/men to surround her/him with true love."

- • "Please help her/him understand the many reasons for her/his SSA."[1]

Build a Prayer Network for Your SSA Child

If you have access to a prayer network, request that its participants actively pray for your son or daughter. And don't be afraid to ask. Sad to say, a lot of parents are ashamed to tell anyone about their child's SSA. The more we postpone being honest, the longer it will take our families to heal. Keeping your child and his problem in the proverbial closet serves no one.

However, if it really is too difficult for you to talk to other people about your child's SSA, ask for generic prayers, such as "God please heal [child's name] heart, mind and soul. Help [child's name] to experience your love and your truth."

In the daily prayers used by devout Jews, the following prayer is said: "Heal us, O Lord, and we shall be healed. Grant a perfect healing to all our wounds." This prayer might be personalized for your SSA child.

---

[1]For Christians, Cindy Rullman's *The Healing Word* has wonderful prayers for SSA children.

"Heal our son, O Lord, and he shall be healed. Grant a perfect healing for all his wounds."

Creative Visualization

When you pray for your child, in your imagination, picture her healed. Use the three Ss of creative visualization as you intercede:

- *See it*: Picture her healed, married, fulfilling her God-given destiny.

- *Say it*: Develop a simple sentence that captures God's desire for your child's life. For example, "God bring Johanna into the fullness of her true femininity and help her fulfill her destiny."

- *Sense it*: Experience how it will feel when you see this dream come true.

You may repeat the same simple sentence each time you pray. Say it over and over again as you envision your child fulfilling her destiny and God's purpose. Do this daily. And as things begin to shift, create a new vision and continue to visualize the healing and fulfillment of the dream.

Father's Prayer of Blessing for Children

The father's patriarchal responsibility is to pass on God's blessing to each of his children (both male and female). Pray for your sons and daughters when they depart or on special occasions. Place your arm around their shoulders, lay your hand on their head or embrace them. In time, your children will begin to associate the warmth of your touch with God's love. They will look forward to your blessings.

A father's blessing may consist of the following elements:[2]

- affirmation of God's plan and promise for your child's life (use Scripture if you like)

---

[2]Suggested books on giving the blessing: William T. Ligon, *Imparting the Blessing to Your Child* (Brunswick, Ga.: The Father's Blessing, 1989), to order call 800-982-9685 or 912-264-0028; and Gary Smalley and John Trent, *The Blessing* (New York: Pocket Books, 1986).

- praise for your child's natural talents, abilities and character
- a request for fulfillment of the desires of your child's heart (goals and aspirations)
- a reminder of the meaning of your child's name and the importance she holds for you, the family and lineage
- a promise of your support for your child's life and dreams

JONAH'S Arthur Goldberg adds, "If you are of the Jewish faith, it is customary to recite the following blessing upon your children—regardless of age—on the eve of the Sabbath and on holy days. If you do not observe this practice, I recommend you do so by placing both hands on your child's head and repeat the following prayer."

> May the Lord make you like Ephraim and Manasseh (to your sons).
> May the Lord make you like Sarah, Rebecca, Rachel and Leah (to your daughters).
> May the Lord bless you and keep you.
> May the Lord cause his presence to shine upon you and be gracious unto you.
> May the Lord turn with favor unto you and give you peace.
> (an adaptation of Numbers 6:24-26)

It may be that your SSA child has denied your spiritual beliefs and rejected God. One reason this may have happened is because your child is detached from you, and you are the earthly, visible manifestation of God. Parents represent the masculine and feminine nature of God. So if the child disconnects from either one of you, then he will naturally disconnect from God. Also, you can be sure that people of different faiths have been extremely punishing and judgmental toward your SSA child. "Homosexuality is the worst sin of all!" is a common statement of judgment and rejection that can be heard in far too many churches and synagogues.

If your child is from a believing home, he may have struggled for years trying to reconcile SSA with Scripture. If he does not come to understand that God loves him regardless of his SSA, he may have had to reject his faith in order to experience the smallest measure of self-worth. The personal torment about his SSA, coupled with the judgmental attitudes of many religious people, compounds his detachment from God and perhaps even his family's religious beliefs. For him, trying to be close to God feels like pain and rejection.

If you keep this in mind, you won't expect your child to readily accept your prayers of blessing. If she is very hurt, it may take a long time for her to allow you to draw closer. No matter what, be persistent and never give up. Your child needs you, even though she feels very angry and hurt. This is the underlying contradictory nature of SSA and all homosexual relationships: "I need you, but don't get too close. Please hold me in your arms. No, it hurts too much. Hey, come back, I want you. Go away. Help, I'm dying in here. Someone please rescue me."

Do Your Best and Let God Do the Rest

By now you've probably come to the conclusion that you are not God. That's not only good, it's also all too true. That's why it is important for you to do all you can to create greater intimacy with your SSA child and then release your child to God's care.

As we've seen, God rarely heals people instantaneously, so you needn't waste your time and prayers on quick fixes. The idea of immediate healing contradicts the process of human growth and development. Restoration of the heart and mind reverses the way the original wounding occurred, and all that took a while. Therefore it is important to listen to your child's story, to hear how she or he journeyed from struggler to "gay" person. Begin with the present and work your way back to the past. You cannot expect to restore over night or even in a few short months the years the locust has eaten (see Joel 2:25). It took months and years to develop SSA. It will take months and years to undo the damage.

In the meantime, be patient with yourself, with your spouse and especially with your child. Give God time to do his perfect work. Call on him for strength, wisdom, understanding and, most of all, love. Do your best. Trust him to do the rest.

Section Two

RELATIONAL HEALING

In section two, you will learn about the many causes of same-sex attractions and what can be done to help SSA children heal and experience the fullness of their innate heterosexuality. Use good communication skills when sharing with and listening to your loved one. Learn about your child's love language. Same-sex parent, you need to spend quality time with your SSA child. Opposite-sex parent, you need to take a backseat for now. It's time to reorder your family's way of living and loving one another.

- Step Four: Investigate the Causes of SSA
- Step Five: Utilize Effective Communication Skills
- Step Six: Make Things Right Between You and Your SSA Child
- Step Seven: Discover Your Child's Love Language
- Step Eight: Same-Sex Parent, Display Appropriate Physical Affection
- Step Nine: Opposite-Sex Parent, Take Two Steps Back

STEP FOUR
Investigate the Causes of SSA

Did you know that there is no such thing as someone simply being a "homosexual"? *Homosexual* is *not* essentially a person's identity—it more properly and rightly describes someone's thoughts, feelings, desires and perhaps behavior. Furthermore, it is not morally wrong to experience a same-sex attraction, because, as we've seen, it represents the soul's attempt to heal wounds and fulfill unmet love needs. SSA becomes a moral issue when someone decides to act on those desires in an unhealthy way. Homosexual behavior is a psychological defense against pain. If you judge a person for having same-sex attraction, you are re-wounding his soul. In fact, you are heaping coals on the fire. This is why it is important to educate yourself, loved ones and a supportive community about the truth of SSA.

JONAH codirector Arthur Goldberg states,

> For those who believe that Leviticus 18:22 creates guilt in those engaging in homosexual behavior, it is useful to point out how the Talmud, written well over 2,000 years ago, explains that the Hebrew word *to'eivah* (translated as an abomination) is an acronym for the words, "You have been led astray." This ancient wisdom makes clear that acting upon the unmet love needs through sexual activity is an error of judgment, and further states that all errors are correctable. Thus, SSA was recognized 2,500 years ago as healable.

We must therefore help people understand the following points:

1. *There is no compelling evidence that anyone is determined from birth to have SSA.* There is no conclusive scientific data that proves there is a simple biological or genetic cause for homosexuality. Scientific research indicates that although biological and genetic factors may play a part, homosexual desires stem from the complex interaction of psychological, environmental and temperament influences along with those factors.

2. *No one simply chooses to have SSA.* These desires are very often the result of unresolved childhood wounds and unmet love needs. Choice is clearly involved in the decision whether or not to act on the desires.

3. *People can be hopeful in their choice to seek a change from a homosexual to a heterosexual orientation.* Research demonstrates that the claim that no one can change is false. Change is possible for some.

4. *There is reason to be hopeful that what is learned can be unlearned.* The path to healing is fourfold: (1) understand the root causes of SSA, (2) gain support from others, (3) fulfill unmet needs for love in healthy, healing, nonsexual relationships with those of the same gender and (4) heal the wounds that created the desires in the first place. After this, opposite-sex desires naturally emerge.

5. *It is not gay or bad; it is SSAD (Same-Sex Attachment Disorder).*[1] There is nothing "gay" about the homosexual lifestyle. In reality, homosexual sex leads to multiple STDs (sexually transmitted diseases) and a high rate of HIV infection. And although it is not "bad" to have same-sex attractions, acting on those desires by engaging in homosexual relationships not only involves high medical risks but also prevents people from gaining the very

---

[1]Richard Cohen, *Coming Out Straight* (Winchester, Va.: Oakhill Press, 2000), p. xi.

things that they are looking for, because their needs are those of a child, not an adult.

Therefore I call this SSAD, or Same-Sex Attachment Disorder. The actual basis for most homosexual desires is a need for bonding and attachment with one's same-sex parent and same-sex peers. Because basic love needs were not met or experienced in early childhood and adolescence, they became eroticized after puberty. Then the world says, "You are gay."

It is a great travesty to label a wounded soul with a sexual identity. SSAD is a cry for help from a wounded child in an adolescent or adult body. Again, when the wounds are healed and the unmet love needs are fulfilled in healthy same-sex relationships, the person will experience the fullness of his own gender identity and opposite-sex desires will ensue. This is why dad and mom and other loved ones are so important: they can play an active part in the resolution of SSA. Anyone who experiences SSA is attempting to bond and attach with someone of the same gender to complete the necessary stages of psychosexual, psychosocial and psychological development.

Several parents I've counseled have been disgusted by the thought of their child being attracted to someone of the same gender. If these are your thoughts and feelings, you will need to make a journey from disgust to compassion. The road to healing is a road of understanding, and it is a long road. The more you understand about SSA, the more quickly you and your family will arrive at the destination of love. Study literature, watch movies, read stories about strugglers and meet others who have experienced SSA. Listen as they share their journey with you. As you learn, your heart will open toward your loved one.

Write an Evaluation of Why You Believe Your Child Has SSA

It is important to understand why your child or loved one experiences SSA. You may ask yourself: "What did I do wrong?" "What did we do wrong?" "Who did this to our child?" Rarely is one thing alone responsible for SSA; it is the result of a combination of variables.

Following is a list of ten factors that may lead to homosexual desires.[2]

1. Heredity. Inherited wounds, unresolved family issues, misinterpretations, a predilection for rejection. At the core of SSA is a sense of not belonging, of not fitting in and of feeling different. These feelings and thoughts may be inherited from one's religious or cultural lineage. This is *not* the same thing as the so-called gay gene. However, these lineage issues may imbue a child with a predilection for rejection.

2. Temperament. Hypersensitivity, high maintenance, artistic nature, gender nonconforming behaviors. If there is anything genetic to SSA, it may be a predisposition to greater sensitivity, whereby the child reacts more deeply than other children to any given situation. Often they are highly attuned to the feelings and emotions of others. They may be more passive and therefore less aggressive in nature. Of course, not all sensitive children will develop SSA.

A child may have an artistic nature and be ostracized for such gifts by either parents, siblings or peers. The child may exhibit gender nonconforming behaviors (for example, he is a boy who plays with dolls and is involved with other feminine activities, or she is an athletic girl who hangs out with boys).

3. Hetero-emotional wounds. Enmeshment (child is overattached to the opposite-sex parent), imitation of that parent's behaviors (the son acts more feminine than masculine, and the daughter acts more masculine than feminine). Sometimes these children feel as if they were born the wrong sex. In many cases, sons with SSA are emotionally entangled with their moms and estranged from their dads. They are inclined to internalize the mother's femininity and are distant from the masculinity that the father represents. The daughter may be closer to her father and

---

estranged from her mother. She then internalizes her father's masculinity and rejects her mother's femininity. In other cases, a son may perceive that his parents wanted a girl. The daughter may believe her parents wanted a boy. They then model their behavior after the opposite sex to please their parents and win their approval and affection.

4. Homo-emotional wounds. Lack of emotional bonding and secure attachment between father and son or mother and daughter; abusive treatment and/or emotional unavailability by the same-sex parent. Homo-emotional wounding is often a core issue with those who experiences SSA. The son did not sufficiently bond with his father or internalize his love and masculinity. The daughter did not sufficiently bond with her mother or internalize her love and femininity. This leads to gender detachment, which lays the groundwork for future same-sex attraction. One of the most devastating things that a child can experience is a father's or mother's emotional unavailability. This can directly impact a child's developing SSA. Remember, highly sensitive children may perceive rejection and then emotionally detach from the same-sex parent. This sense of being rejected may completely reside in the child's mind and not be part of your reality at all.

5. Sibling wounds/family dynamics. Put-downs, abusive treatment, name-calling. Often SSA boys are at odds with their brothers or believe they cannot measure up to them. They may be called names or experience physical abuse from siblings or same-sex relatives. These sensitive children are often people-pleasers, trying to iron out all the difficulties between other family members. I have heard from countless parents, "My son was the perfect little boy, a perfect gentleman." Be careful of those "good little boys." Boys are not meant to be so sweet and kind as they are often, by nature, assertive, gregarious and mischievous.

6. Body image wounds. A late bloomer; a child with physical disabilities or illness; a girl who is athletically precocious; a boy who is athletically challenged; children who are unusually short or tall, thin or overweight;

kids with poor eye-hand coordination. Many SSA youth feel inadequate about their physical appearance and/or lack of gender prowess. Since they have detached from their same-sex parent and have perhaps experienced rejection from same-sex siblings and/or same-sex peers, they most likely have also become detached from their own gender identity. The result is a profound sense of gender inadequacy. If they were late bloomers, they felt different and alienated from their peers. Being shorter or taller than their peers may have compounded their sense of alienation. I have heard many SSA men state, "I was always the last one picked for the team during gym class." In turn, this may have affected their ability to bond with same-sex peers, always being the odd man out.

7. *Sexual abuse.* Homosexual imprinting and patterning based on having been sexually abused. Same-sex activity may become a learned and reinforced behavior, a poor substitute for genuine love and affection. Many who experience SSA were sexually abused as children or adolescents. Kids are more susceptible to abuse if they don't experience warmth and affection from their same-sex parent and/or same-sex peers. Sex then becomes a replacement for emotional and relational intimacy with others of the same gender. This pattern of sexual behavior is reinforced over time and becomes a predictor for the development of SSA. (Warning: please don't assume that your child was sexually abused if she or he struggles with SSA. Abuse is just one of many contributing factors, not a prerequisite for having same-sex attraction.)

8. *Homo-social wounds.* Name-calling, rejection on the playground, mocking over appearance, disability or some other different characteristic. Many boys and girls experience a tremendous sense of emotional wounding because of same-sex peer rejection. They do not fit in and are called names (for example, "sissy," "faggot," "queer," "dyke," "lessy," "tomboy"). Often the boys are more comfortable with female friends and shy away from typical male activities. When they "come out," instantaneously they are surrounded by a welcoming community of others who,

like themselves, did not fit in. Misery loves company.

9. Cultural wounds. Social indoctrination by media, educational systems, political organizations, entertainment, academia and the Internet—born gay and cannot change, the "innate, immutable" concept. Today our youth are being solicited into homosexuality under false pretenses. It is actually becoming quite trendy to be "gay" or "bi." These myths are enrolling young, impressionable and vulnerable children into a lifestyle that will ultimately betray them.

Many children are growing up in single-parent families and crave attention and affection from a same-sex mentor or peer. The need for emotional bonding with a same-sex parent and same-sex peers becomes sexualized through adolescence as an attempt to meet legitimate love needs. The media, educational systems and the entertainment industry now create a false identity called "gay." *There is no such thing as "gay"; there are only hurt children looking for love.*

10. Other factors. Divorce, death of a parent, adoption, religion, rejection by opposite-sex peers. A sensitive child may perceive it as a personal rejection if a parent dies or there is divorce in the family. This may contribute to his sense of gender confusion. When religious doctrine condemns homosexuality and children experience same-sex attraction through no fault of their own, a tremendous weight of guilt and shame is placed on their shoulders. How could a loving God do such a thing? Also, if a child is detached from his parents, he will most often reject his parents' "God" or religious beliefs.

An adopted child may feel rejected by the birth parents and never securely attached to the new family. This sense of rejection may reside deep in the unconscious, creating a pattern of insecurity.

And finally, a boy with an already fragile sense of gender identity (or lack thereof) may experience rejection when trying to court or date a girl. Her refusal further distances him from feeling like a man.

Caught in a Double Bind

These are some of the contributing factors that may lead to the development of SSA in men and women. When several factors combine to form
the underlying causes of SSA, a pattern emerges where individuals find
themselves in a "gender double bind." Psychotherapist David Matheson
writes about this phenomenon:

> A double bind is a situation where there is no good way out—
> where there is pain or trouble no matter what you do. . . . One of
> the worst double binds these boys experience is being taught that
> it is bad to be a boy. This can be called *gender double bind*. If they
> assert their masculinity, they are punished. If they abandon it, they
> experience a deep sense of loss which, lacking any help from the
> environment to absorb, they repress, and cover up—often through
> sexual behavior. Gender double binds are created by mothers (and
> sometimes fathers) who express disapproval of males and mascu-
> linity, or praise their boy for being different from other boys.[3]

The essence of this gender double bind is that a man is not okay with being
a man, nor is he okay with not being a man. He sees no way out. He is
caught between two worlds, with nowhere to turn. One side of his psyche
says, "I am a man," but the other side says, "I am not accepted as a masculine person, so I'm not really a man. Something is missing within me."

Peter and Barbara Wyden point out in *Growing Up Straight* that one
key factor in this catch-22 is the influence of the father:

> Experts do agree that the role of fathers is one of the principal
> problems—possibly even the number one problem—in homosex-
> uality; that mothers have perhaps been blamed too much over the
> years; that the significance of fathers, in the making of male as well

---

[3]David Matheson, "Four Principles of Change: A Supplement for the Journey into Manhood
Weekend" (2003), pp. 3-4.

as female homosexuality, has been inadequately recognized; and that parents should develop a better understanding of why this is a crucial factor.[4]

Dr. Judd Marmor puts it this way: "For a homosexual adaptation to occur, in our time and culture, these factors must combine to (1) create an impaired gender-identity [feeling of masculinity or femininity], (2) create a fear of intimate contact with members of the opposite sex, and (3) provide opportunities for sexual release with members of the same sex."[5]

Dr. Joseph Nicolosi teaches about the unhealthy triadic relationship in the pre-homosexual family system. The sensitive son is overattached to his mother, quite distant from his father and rejected by same-sex peers.[6]

Struggler's Teleconferencing Classes have been a lifeline for a man in Beijing, as there are no local resources in his country. He made the following observations:

Sometimes I watch the street boys play. They are "bad boys," smoking and calling each other bad names. I see they have intimate behaviors with each other, such as hugging, touching each other, and so on. They look tough, not sissy or gay. So I think it is normal for boys and males to have intimate relationships when growing up, so that a boy can fully know he is a boy among boys, and he will not grow up to be gay.

I saw some teenagers playing with each other at the swimming pool. They ride on each other's shoulders, hug each other from behind, and hold the other's chest and waist. They touch each other's private parts and even see it and joke. They seem to like to touch each other's upper bodies, and there is nothing sexual about it, but

---

[4]Peter and Barbara Wyden, *Growing Up Straight* (New York: Stein and Day, 1968), p. 18.
[5]Ibid., p. 19.
[6]Joseph and Linda Ames Nicolosi, *A Parent's Guide to Preventing Homosexuality* (Downers Grove, Ill.: InterVarsity Press, 2002).

being brave and rude and intimate. It seems to be something they like and need. Meanwhile they need other things, such as girls.

I think when someone knows what he has, he will feel no lack. If he feels he lacks something, he will feel eager to get it and be attracted to it. If a person is forced to study and stay away from outdoor activities with other boys, he will admire the life of sailors and construction workers. He will like their strong manner and suntanned skin. On the other hand, the educated one feels a lack of confidence, that he has no knowledge of men and is useless.[7]

Insightful. And painful too, when you put yourself in his situation. He is an amazing man. In the many years I have known him, he has made remarkable progress. Actually he is now married and has his first child. When we started working together, he did not have a clue about SSA. He just knew it was wrong for him. He is a great student and has done the necessary work to heal and grow.

In the International Healing Foundation's Struggler's Teleconferencing Class, I ask participants to evaluate the causes of their SSA based on the ten variables we looked at above. Here are two such examples.

Bonnie's Evaluation

Heredity. My family was dysfunctional in many ways. We are of German descent, and there was not a lot of affection, but coolness. There was perfectionism in my mother's family, a sense of never being able to measure up, not being good enough. I also believe I was predisposed to depression, as my mother and her mother dealt with it also.

Temperament. I never had thick skin; words and negative attitudes were hurtful. I cried easily and still do, but received little consolation. Rather, "I'll give you something to cry about" was often ex-

---

[7]Used with permission of the writer.

pressed. I was also a "tomboy," as was my mother. This was not discouraged but almost encouraged, as my parents bought me boys' toys like soldiers and toy guns. I had two older brothers, and their friends were my friends. I was the only girl among them. I was not comfortable in girl's clothing and hated dresses and pantyhose. When I did experiment with makeup, my father made fun of me and asked if I was putting on "war paint."

Hetero-emotional wounds. I do not recall my father ever once saying he loved me. I do not recall him ever telling me I was pretty. He never said I was ugly, but when I became overweight, he'd say that I'd find some boyfriend who liked "a lot to squeeze." He never treated me special. I had a cousin on my mother's side whose father seemed to adore her. He called her princess, and he doted on her. I was jealous. I do not feel I was close to my father. He provided for us, paid the bills, but he was emotionally closed. He was not close to my brothers either. He made things for us, but he was not demonstrative and warm.

Homo-emotional wounds. My mother and I were enmeshed. She would often unburden her heart to me over many personal problems, even when I was only ten or so. I felt responsible for her feelings, for taking care of her. Yet I also felt rejected by her. She used to be affectionate, but it stopped almost overnight, and I wondered what I had done that made my mother stop loving me. And the worst was the sexual abuse I experienced. There is a very clear incident I can testify to that she did when I was eight, but my body remembers earlier things, as early as three—things in the bathtub, times when she punished me for sex play with my friends by making me do sexual things with her. I know that much of my lesbian behavior was a reenactment of some of those things, only then I had control and was able to please the other woman.

Sibling wounds. My brothers, well, they could be awful, especially the one who is five years older than I. He did not play with me or protect me. He did not seem like he wanted me around. When my parents left us alone, he and my other brother, fourteen months older than I, would pick on me terribly and tease me until I cried. They never said I was pretty or introduced me to their boyfriends. They told me not to tell the girls at school I was their sister. Sometimes they would tell me I was adopted. They made fun of me because I was fat and cried easily.

Body image wounds. I have been obese since puberty and unable to lose weight. My parents were accepting of that, as they too were obese, but others did not like me, at least not at first. I had to work hard to make a friend, to get them to see beyond my body. I hated having a period. I hated being touched sexually, and having a woman's genitalia was nothing but trouble.

Sexual abuse. I was also molested by a few men in my life: At age eight by a train conductor who touched me inappropriately while we were all on a family trip; by a friend of my girlfriend's father, who fondled me; and by a sixty-five-year-old partially blind man I was helping as part of a scouting project. He and I often kissed, and he fondled me. I was thirteen and felt responsible for that until I was in my forties. There were others. I never had intercourse or oral sex with a man, but there were enough instances of unwelcome sexual contact to make me suspicious and fearful.

Homo-social wounds. I was not comfortable with girls my age, but did better with girls a few years younger. Actually I had few female friends and spent a lot of time visiting our elderly neighbors because they listened to me. In high school I found a group of girls who were also not part of the "in crowd," and we formed our own little clique. We are still friends, for which I am thankful, but it was not enough to overcome all the other wounds!

Other factors. I know for a fact that my parents did not want me. They had two children, and my mother conceived me when my brother was only about five months old. It was traumatic for her, and

I do not think my father wanted me either. I also heard my mother tell my aunt that she was disappointed I was a girl.[8]

Adrian's Evaluation

Heredity. My father was emotionally distant. He remained aloof from both my sister and me because of his personal problems with his own father. I was therefore distanced from all extended family males. My mother was eccentric, needy and desperate for attention. Actually her side of the family was weird. Both my parents distanced themselves from their families when they started their own family.

Temperament. I am highly sensitive, very artistic, a people-pleaser. I do exactly what I am told and then some, always performing and giving others what I think they want. I get perfect grades, have perfect handwriting and am neat and clean. I take care of everyone else before myself.

Hetero-emotional wounds. All the women in my life wore the pants. I was very close to my mother, but she abandoned me millions of times (she never picked me up from school, dance classes or anything on time). She ruined many things because of her over-the-top personality. She does things without asking me, making final decisions about my life. All hetero-relationships for me are love-hate relationships.

Homo-emotional wounds. My father oftentimes ignored me. The only emotion he showed besides indifference was *anger*. He forced me to do sports that he coached, and I hated it. I would rather have been playing dolls with my sister or putting on a dress or something. Neither of my parents came to my shows or swim meets on a regular basis. My dad just watched TV, and that is basically what our relationship was about.

Sibling wounds. My sister had a disability, so I was launched into

---

[8]Bonnie has forgiven her mother and is flourishing in her life. She is married and now leads a ministry that assists others in healing from unwanted SSA.

the role of older brother, caretaker and best friend. I could not have any friends of my own. She made me feel guilty a lot. I couldn't have a mind of my own, because I felt like I always needed to agree with her and just be her friend.

Body image wounds. I am very tall but never felt proud of my height. I feel lanky, gangly, skinny and pale. I have red hair and blond eyebrows that everyone notices, and it always bothers me. I never liked my teeth, and I had severe acne for a long time.

Homo-social wounds. I suffered from name-calling and had no friends of the same sex. I just wanted to fit in. I was a goody-goody, a teacher's pet, a flatterer. I was involved in zero boy activities.

Cultural wounds. I was a media junkie. I loved TV. The dance culture is a gay culture, so I was exposed to everything and all different kinds of people. For example, our whole dance company would go to a gay bar.

Educational system. All my good teachers were female. I never had a male teacher I liked or respected. My male peers were verbally abusive to me, and I was treated like a girl.

Internet. I had a porn addiction for a while.

Other factors. I was the pastor's kid, so I had to perform even more in front of the parishioners. The only rule of our family was to show up for church.[9]

Remember, SSA is always a symptom of unresolved childhood wounds and unmet needs for love. It may be hard at first, but begin to investigate your child's wounds and needs. Using these ten factors, make a list of the reasons why you believe your child experiences SSA. *Do not show this evaluation to your child.* This is strictly for your reference as parents in order to discover how best to love your child and how to assist in the process of healing. Both of you may write an evaluation indepen-

---

[9]Adrian is well on his way to healing, taking the necessary steps toward fulfilling his true masculine identity.

dently of the other and then share your lists with each other.

I know this exercise of writing down the multiple reasons for your child's SSA may evoke strong emotions. Allow yourself time to grieve. Get support from your spouse and friends. Express your feelings with others, not just alone. This will help you heal quicker and be more available for your spouse and children. Take your time.

Develop a Library of Materials About SSA

Build a library of useful materials about the causes and healing of homosexuality. Also, learn about the homosexual movement and its activities. It is important to know what your child is learning, so you can see through his eyes, understand his world. (Please refer to the resources at the end of this book for recommended reading and websites.)

It is important for you to read pro-homosexual materials so you may gain an understanding of your child's way of thinking. But please, do so only when you feel strong, because such materials can stir up chaos in your soul. They may make you furious, outraged and sick to your stomach. Remember, the "gay" activists and their allies have been at this for decades. They have time, money, personnel and resources. They are, for the most part, single men and women with high incomes, no children and lots of time on their hands. They are driven by anger, resentment and pain. Their demands represent life and death for them: they put their lives on the line every day because they want and need our acceptance. The problem is, they are unaware of the truth about SSA. So once again, read their websites and literature when you feel emotionally stable. This fact-finding investigation is for your education; therefore do not share with or show this information to your SSA child. I will explain more about this in step six.

Finding a Therapist

Please don't insist that your child see a therapist unless she has a desire to

pursue change. When that time comes, do not take your child to a therapist unless you have thoroughly investigated his or her credentials and
success rate in dealing with SSA. You may do more harm than good if you
allow your child to see someone who has little or no experience in this
area. You also do not want to subject her to someone who will simply try
to "pray" this away or "cast out demons." I know of several cases where
parents brought their children to a religious person who tried to "de-pos-
sess" them. It was an immediate turn-off for the SSA child.

Please keep in mind what has been stated before about "gay affirmative" therapists. This is the default position of the mental health profession and recovery movement. In fact, they have given a new diagnosis to
those who do not accept their homosexuality: "internalized homopho-
bia." This means that if the client does not accept his SSA, then he has
internalized societal or religious prejudice toward homosexuality. So be
careful when selecting a therapist.

Once you and your child decide that the time has come to seek help,
here are some questions you might consider asking a prospective therapist:

- What is your education and training in the areas of same-sex attrac-
  tion and reorientation therapy?
- What is your personal belief about homosexuality and SSA?
- Do you practice or believe in "gay affirmative therapy"? (It is important to ask this question. Don't make any assumptions when inter-
  viewing therapists, even if they are religious.)
- How long have you been helping people heal from unwanted SSA?
- Have you been successful in helping men and women transition from
  a homosexual to a heterosexual orientation?
- What kind of success rate do you have?
- Have you had personal experience with SSA? (Like me, some therapists have come out of homosexuality; however, that is not a require-
  ment for a good therapist.)

- If you were to work with my child, what therapeutic approaches would you use? (To understand more about therapeutic approaches, read chapters four and six of *Coming Out Straight*.)
- If it is important to you: Do you believe in God?

Even if therapists claim to have a personal faith in God, don't assume it means that they understand SSA. Many Christian and Jewish therapists also believe in the "innate, immutable" concept of homosexuality. Also, some therapists will say they can help your child in dealing with SSA, but they still believe in "gay affirmative therapy." Please be direct and ask them if they practice this type of therapy.

You may want to consider family versus individual therapy. SSA is a systemic issue and healing may be accelerated by involving the entire family—dad, mom and all the children. This way, the focus is not on the child with SSA, but everyone gets to participate in family healing. If you choose to go this route, be sure to find a competent therapist who has experience working with families. This is an art in itself, and many therapists are not comfortable with or have no training in family therapy.

Movie Therapy

There is much to learn about the culture by observing art. Art imitates life, and today, because there are so many SSA men and women in the entertainment industry, life is imitating art. I have rented dozens of movies with homosexual themes written, directed or produced by SSA men and women. These films are the best testimonies about the unhappiness and misery of the SSAD condition. They teach us how lonely and unfulfilling a homosexual life actually is. Be forewarned: if you rent any of these movies, it may cause you or other family members emotional pain and unrest. Consider watching one or more of the following movies, but do so with a loved one (not your SSA child), and share about your thoughts and feelings afterward.

- *The Deep End.* The mother is overprotective, indulging her son while the father is away at sea, and the son hungers for his father's love. This is a typical triadic relationship: sensitive and artistic son, overattachment to mom, distant from dad.

- *Breaking the Surface: The Greg Louganis Story.* Again, the typical triadic family relationship is depicted. Olympic gold medal diver Greg Louganis is an adopted child with an abusive father and an overprotective mother. The sensitive son tries desperately to obtain his father's love through athletic achievement and finally in abusive relationships with other men.

- *Latter Days.* A disturbing commentary about religious rejection of those with SSA, this movie shows the great harm that comes from ignorance. This is the story of a Mormon missionary repressing his SSA and being seduced by a "gay" man. It shows his parents' reacting in all the wrong ways—with judgment and condemnation. They send him to a horrific program to "cure" him, but he ends up running back to his boyfriend.

- *Angels in America.* This 2003 Emmy-winning HBO drama by Pulitzer Prize-winning playwright Tony Kirshner is a truly tragic story of tormented SSA souls seeking solace and comfort from one another as they confront the onset of AIDS in the 1980s. There is no hope or redemption offered. The author has no understanding about the true nature of SSA and the potential for change.

- *Normal.* This 2003 HBO movie portrays a man who believes he was born in the wrong body and sets out to change his gender from male to female after twenty-five years of marriage. Again, it shows no understanding about gender identity disorder. There is a brief allusion to the relationship with his dad—shaming, name-calling, verbal abuse.

- *Brokeback Mountain.* This Oscar-winning 2005 film depicts the unhappiness of two very confused cowboys. The movie sadly leaves out the unfulfilling life they would have had if they'd lived together. Both parties are wounded and looking for the same thing that neither one of them had experienced: healthy parental love.

• *Queer as Folk* and *The L Word.* These two Showtime series depict the ephemeral lifestyle of men and women engaged in homosexual activity. Watch these shows only when you feel strong. They will evoke emotions of disgust, shock and pain.

On the other hand, there are many beautiful films that will give you some ideas about healing parent-child relationships and creating an alliance of love: *Frequency, Field of Dreams, Man of the House* (the older version with Chevy Chase and Farrah Fawcett), *Life as a House, The Karate Kid,* Disney's *The Kid, The Chosen, The Man Without a Face, Down in the Delta, Coach Carter* and *Good Will Hunting.*

Tom's Story

Films and fiction teach us many lessons. But real life is where the truth resides. In the following first-person account, you will see into the heart of one of my clients. When he came to me several years ago, he was strictly attracted to men. Now opposite-sex desires are emerging, and he is getting ready to date women.

> *Out of the forthright admission of one's frailties and the determined commitment to go on, comes a laminated strength powerful enough to overcome those who have not made such a struggle.*
>
> **LAWRENCE LERNER, "FANTASTIC"**

By the time, at age thirty-two, I began to seriously address my SSA, I had been struggling with it for so long I could barely remember life without it. There are no words to adequately express how consuming and crippling it was. As I write this, I am thirty-five and continuing on my journey of recovery, moving toward the reclamation of my true masculine potential which lay dormant for so long. Although two and a half years have passed since I decided to finally confront my SSA, the start of this journey seems like it was a lifetime ago. In some ways, it was.

It all began when I was six years old. My father was at that time a raging alcoholic, my older brother (seven years older than I) was rebelling against him, and my mother was desperately trying to hold our family together. At about this time I started school, and I began to see how other kids behaved with their parents and how life appeared to be in their homes. I was and am a very sensitive person, very quick to read the surroundings and underlying mood of a situation. I recognized quickly that something was not entirely right in our home, not only with my father but with our entire family. As the years went on, it was very painful to watch my father deteriorate into his addiction, and along with him our family life deteriorated too.

When I was ten, my mother gave my father an ultimatum: "Stop drinking or I am leaving you." He did stop, and never touched a drink again. Although the nights of wondering if my father would come home drunk ended, I still never felt comfortable with him. Particularly in the early years of his sobriety, it was as if our family was playing a game of make-believe, as if the turmoil caused by his drinking—or the anticipation of that turmoil—had never existed. To this day, my father has never once acknowledged that he was ever wrong. Even after nearly twenty-five years of sobriety, he cannot speak of his drinking days, and worse, he takes no responsibility for them.

As I've grown and come to better understand my father, I recognize that he is in many ways what Alcoholics Anonymous calls a "dry drunk," someone who is no longer drinking but whose thinking is still distorted by the thought patterns of addiction. I also recognized very early on that I would rather die than be like him. It gives me no pleasure to say that; it is in fact profoundly sad to do so. But it is true. While my father was staying sober, my brother—with whom he never got along—was going his own way. My brother had the unique ability to infuriate our father on many occasions. Why couldn't he just shut up and keep the peace? I made the decision somewhere around the age of thirteen that I was never going to be like my brother either.

Male dad angry

During those turbulent years, the one thing I wanted more than anything else was to protect my mother. In my view, she'd been through enough. My father's insensitivity to her, the stress she took on mediating between my brother and father, the pain the entire situation caused her—it was too much. I vowed that I would never hurt her. I would be the perfect son. In the process I became her sounding board, in a sense her emotional "husband." To say I became overly attached to her is an understatement.

Meanwhile I was discovering that my extreme sensitivity and lack of athletic ability in a hyper-masculine hometown were crippling me. I did not fit in with the other boys. I was passive, afraid to fight. I liked to dress nicely, and I was weak and overweight. I felt in some ways, really in many ways, crushed by the circumstances of my life. I wanted to be someone else. By this time I was thirteen, in the spring of the seventh grade, my SSA began.

The first boy I became attracted to was a year older than I, and he was everything I could have been "if only." He was smart, athletic, preppy and seemed very nice. At that point I didn't consciously think it was weird for me to be constantly thinking about this guy. What I remember asking myself was, *How can I be more like him? How can I turn into him? How can I get him to like me?*

As I entered high school, I re-experienced those feelings for other boys. They were always the same—lean, preppy, baby-faced, safe. I studied how they dressed and acted, what they liked and tried to emulate them. Above all else, I worked hard to get them to like me and be my closest friends. The tension and excitement that this all-consuming quest caused me cannot be overstated. I often masturbated while thinking about them, trying to relieve the anxiety that all of those feelings caused. Yet I remained in deep denial about the nature of my feelings.

In the rare moments when I reflected on what I was doing, I recognized that it was highly unlikely that these boys, whom I so admired, felt the same way about me. But this didn't stop me—my emotional cravings and need for belonging were too strong. Time after time, no matter what guy I pursued, obsessed over and longed to be with, every single time I got my heart broken in some way. Nothing ever worked out the way I wanted it to. Before long I would turn my attention toward someone else, and the same thing would happen all over again.

My religious tradition was Roman Catholic, and my SSA feelings were a source of guilt and shame to me. I had "girlfriends," but only because it was what was expected of me. I would never have admitted to anyone that my feelings for guys were stronger and more intense than what I felt for girls. It was an exercise in stamina and required tremendous acting to pretend that I was "normal."

In the summer between seventh and eighth grades, a man I had come to trust and tried to emulate offered me a ride home from an event. I was shocked when he started asking me questions about how often I masturbated, how I did it and whether I liked it. His questions made me extremely uncomfortable, but I wanted his attention too much to say so. Then, after a few minutes of this kind of talk, he softly said, "Show me how you do it."

It has been twenty-one years since this incident took place, and I still cannot adequately explain the fear I experienced in that moment. Why did I accommodate him? Why did I do what he asked? Because I was afraid—too afraid not to. I was afraid that if I didn't do what he wanted, he wouldn't like me anymore.

As I complied with his request and pulled down my pants, he took one look at me and then began to mock and laugh. I was humiliated beyond words. Even more confusing, minutes later, as he continued to drive me home, he kept talking about nothing in particular, as if the incident never had happened. In the months and years to come I saw this man frequently and he never again asked me to do such a thing. But what he did, which was perhaps even more devastating, was continue to belittle me as he had done during the incident.

I promised myself not to speak of that event to anyone—never, ever. I tried to put it out of my mind, but for the next two decades I carried it within me, feeling deep shame and confusion. As I got older, I heard about other boys who'd had absolutely horrifying experiences of sexual abuse over long periods of time. I tried to convince myself that my own experience was really nothing—a moment too insignificant to remember. But in my heart I knew that simply wasn't true.

Meanwhile, even as I tried to pursue a normal life, my attraction to guys continued. There were still girlfriends too, but as soon as our relationships led to intimacy, whether physical or emotional, an automatic barrier closed in around me. Finally, after "fooling myself" for a couple of years, when I was twenty-four I concluded it was very likely that I was gay.

Now I actively began to seek out other gays. I wanted to explore my feelings further, even though I felt almost nauseated every time I did so. Gradually my emotional attachments to men turned into physical relationships. Every time it happened, I came away more sad, confused, lonelier than ever and sickened by my behavior. I tried to convince myself that everything was okay, but something inside me knew very well that it was not.

This pattern of playing straight while having a double life went on for the next three years, until the night I met the man who would ultimately set me on the path to self-recovery. He was the ultimate combination of all the qualities I had sought for the past fourteen years. He was impossibly good-looking, preppy, baby-faced, physically unimposing—everything I had ever desired in one package. I fell not into love but into an obsession that I now shudder to think about. I clearly remember thinking, *If I could win his friendship, my life would be complete.* I was convinced that, with him beside me, my life of longing and loneliness would be over.

For the next year and a half, I pursued him with sick determination. And every time I went out of my way to prove myself to him, every time I sacrificed, every time I drove past by his house in the middle of the night, I knew deep inside that I was in serious trouble. To the best of my knowledge, he never knew the extent of my feelings. Or maybe he did. The point is my yearnings were never reciprocated. Worse than that, I got the feeling he didn't really care at all.

The pain was crippling. I could never stop thinking about him, and to alleviate my obsession, I impulsively went out in the middle of the night to hook up sexually with the first guy I could find. This went on for months, until one winter night, I sat down alone in my apartment, lonelier and more isolated than I had ever been. I cried bitterly, thinking of the wreckage my life had become, thinking of all the men I had pursued, especially over the last year. I wrote down a vow that I fully intended to keep, even if I didn't know how to do so. All I knew was that this emotional torture could not go on. *This will never happen again,* I promised myself.

Of course my SSA desires continued despite my best intentions. For the next few years, I emotionally cut myself off, despite the fact that I occasionally slipped up and hooked up when the craving became too strong. Three years after I made my vow, and after I repeatedly broke it without really wanting to, I admitted to myself that I needed help.

But my fear of seeking help was overwhelming. What would I find out if I actually talked to someone about my life? Was I truly gay? Was there any hope for change? I continued to struggle with these questions for close to a year. At last, shattered by one more intolerable relationship, I finally did a search on the Web for some kind of an organization that could help men like me. I found the International Healing Foundation website, where I read, "No one is born with SSA."

That was it. I had been right all along. I wasn't supposed to be gay.

Then I read Richard Cohen's book *Coming Out Straight*. I identified with so much of what he wrote and recognized in myself several of the causes of SSA that he listed. I learned that I was a classic SSA male—extremely sensitive, with an alcoholic and abusive father, a very close connection to my mother and a history of sexual abuse. This confirmed what I had always suspected, that my SSA feelings did not happen by accident. After wrestling with my fears a little longer, I made an appointment to talk to Richard.

I thought we could figure all this out in his office, just between the two of us, until he stressed to me the importance of reaching out to other people. Tell other people? He had to be kidding. But he affirmed and reaffirmed this necessity, until I finally agreed to try. *You'd better be right about this,* I warned him.

Before long I discovered that I was blessed with a handful of men in my life with whom I could share the most intimate details of what I'd been through. These men were fantastic. I kept them and Richard captive for hours on end, talking through the heartaches, disappointments and failures I had never talked about to anyone before. It was radical for me to open up like this.

Meanwhile Richard explained that I had to spend the next year reconnecting to my inner child—the wounded little boy within me. Now, at first I thought this was crazy. I did not sense any connection to any child, inner or otherwise. But I slowly realized that it was indeed my inner child who had to be healed, not the thirty-three-year-old adult. This process was not easy, and it took a lot of time for me to connect with my inner child, because "he" had been hurt so deeply. I learned that I had to become a loving father to him—the kind of father I'd never had. Only in doing so could I overcome the lifelong pain, fear and loneliness that had led to my SSA. As I followed this healing path, slowly but surely my SSA feelings started to disappear.

Other difficult issues arose. Confronting the man who had humiliated me became necessary. Looking back, I am still surprised that I was so gung-ho, because being confrontational has never been part of my nature. When the moment finally came, seventeen months after I started my healing of SSA, I can honestly say that I have never felt God's power more strongly than I did as I spoke to him. As empowering as that experience was, it was still only a part of the larger process of setting things right.

I wish I could say the attempts I made in connecting with my father had gone well too, but I learned something I had never considered: that I had the courage and insight to confront my demons, even if he could not. This process of confrontation, of setting things in order, of dealing with the pain, of listening to my inner child, of sharing with other men and of embracing what I felt was my true nature, slowly but surely took away the underlying fear I had of "losing myself."

At last I am getting to know the man that I was truly meant to be.

As I write this, I am in what Richard calls "stage four" of the healing journey. My next step is to speak about these things with my mother and heal my opposite-sex wounds. I am not sure how it will turn out, but I am not worried. I hope to start dating women soon, and I believe that I will.

The healing process takes a lot of time. You cannot rush something like coming out of SSA. But I can say with certainty that I cannot imagine returning to my past behaviors. I *know* change is possible. I am living proof.[10]

---

[10]Used with permission of the writer.

STEP FIVE

Utilize Effective
Communication Skills

In your efforts to reach out in love to your SSA son or daughter, one of the most important aspects of creating intimacy is using good communication skills. Most of us have a lot to learn about the art of communication—especially when we are emotionally involved—because these skills do not come naturally and require practice. Too many of us were never properly schooled in the art of listening and sharing. You may find it helpful to practice some of the skills that follow with your spouse or with your other children and friends. Later on, if the conversations with your SSA child get heated, you will be better prepared to communicate effectively.

One key to good communication that is particularly helpful is reflective listening: paraphrasing what someone says and empathizing with his thoughts and feelings. And please allow me to answer a question before you ask it: no, reflective listening does not mean that you *agree* with what the other person is saying. It simply means that you *understand* where he is coming from and that you care and are using good listening skills. Bad communication is, "I'm right and you're wrong." Good communication is, "I understand your thoughts and feelings and you understand mine." This doesn't imply agreement; it signifies respect and compassion.

Many parents have told me that it is difficult for them to discuss homosexual issues with their child. The proverbial elephant is in the room, but no one is talking about it. By using good communication skills, you will learn how to engage in healthy dialogue about SSA. You may ask open-ended questions such as, "When did you begin to experience same-sex attractions?" Then use reflective listening to continue the conversation. This way you do not have to react defensively or take your child's responses personally. This will help bring your communication to a deeper level.

If there is to be a confrontation, it is essential for you to choose your battles wisely. Always move the conversation toward thoughts, feelings and needs, and away from judgmental statements. Most of us don't want advice but long to be heard and understood. When you wisely apply the following skills, your child will be reassured of your love.

Be a Good Listener

The following are skills to help you become an effective listener:

1. **Make eye contact.** It is important to look into the eyes of the one who is speaking to you. This demonstrates your attentiveness and concern.

2. **Observe body language, tone and words.** More important than words are body language and the tone of expression. That is why eye contact is essential. You can perceive more about people from their facial expressions, gestures and movements than from their words.

3. **Let silence have its place.** Silence is one of the greatest gifts you can give to another person. Do not fill the empty moments with words; just "be" with your child. Sitting with him in the silent moments lets him know that you are "there" for him, and it gives him the opportunity to go deeper into his thoughts and feelings.

4. **Join them.** Rather than give your opinion, step into the other person's shoes and see from his point of view. This is accomplished through reflective listening, in which you paraphrase what he says and hypothesize about how she thinks and feels. Here are three steps to develop re-

flective listening, summarized from Dr. Harville Hendrix's Imago Therapy training seminars:

a. Paraphrase words in small increments. Listen as your child shares a few sentences. Then reflect back what you just heard and add, "Is that right?" or "Did I get it right?" If you happen to be wrong, do not worry; he will correct you. If you left something out, he will tell you. Then paraphrase once again, until you get it right. Then say, "Is there more?" Listen and reflect once again. Keep paraphrasing and asking, "Is there more?" When he says, "No, that's all I have to say," then summarize the basic contents of what you heard. Then say, "Is that basically what you said?" This may take a lot of time. Be patient.

Do not put your own thoughts, feelings or inflection into your reflective listening. It is okay to disagree 100 percent. You just need to *join* with him and reflect what you heard. In this way, he feels understood, regarded and respected.

Example:
He says: "I am tired of you trying to fix me or cure me of my homosexuality."

You say: "It seems like you are tired of me trying to fix or cure you of your homosexuality. Is that it?"

He says: "Yes! That's it. I don't want you to fix me. I'm fine just the way I am. Please, Dad, would you just love me as a gay person and leave it at that?"

You say: "You don't want me to fix you, you're fine the way you are, and all you really need from me is to love you as a gay person and leave it at that."

He says: "Yes, Dad, I think you're finally getting it. I'm your son. I know you love me. I just need you to accept me for who I am."

You say: "You're my son, you know that I love you, and you need me to accept you just the way you are. Is that it, Son?"

He says: "Yes, Dad, that's it. Thank you for listening and understanding me."

You joined him. You met him where he lives. Instead of sharing your personal thoughts, feelings and desires, you joined with his. This takes a lot of practice and patience.

You then summarize: "What I heard you say is that you're tired of me trying to fix or cure you of your homosexuality and that you've been hurt because I didn't accept you just the way you are. And what you really need from me is my love and for me to accept you as a gay man. Is that it?"

He says: "Yes, Dad, you got it."

b. *Empathize with thoughts.* "What you're saying makes sense to me because . . ." Here you have to imagine how he thinks, again by stepping into his shoes. You are validating his thoughts, not agreeing with them. After you finish, say, "Is that right?" If it is wrong, don't worry. He will correct you. Then paraphrase what he says and finish by saying, "Is that the way you think?" When you get an affirmative response, move on to the next step.

Example:

You say: "You make sense to me because you believe that you were born gay, and that that is who you are. There is no difference between Tim as my son and Tim as a gay man. They are one in the same. So your need from me is to accept you as a gay man, without trying to change you. Is that your thinking? Did I get it?"

He says: "Yes, Dad, you do get it. I am born gay, and that's the way it is. So your trying to 'change' me doesn't make sense at all. Being gay is who I am."

You say: "So being gay is who you are. You believe it's the way you were born, so any efforts to 'change' you don't make sense. Is that it? Is there more?"

He says: "No, Dad. You really got it. Thanks for understanding."

c. Empathize with feelings. "Given all that, I imagine you feel . . ." Use simple, feeling words, such as sad, mad, glad, afraid, guilty, ashamed, happy, disappointed, confused. Again, do not worry if you are wrong. Your child will correct you. Then repeat what you heard. "Oh, so you feel . . ." When you get confirmation, you are finished. Congratulations. You have now successfully listened to and honored the one you heard. This is how effective listening takes place. It is a skill that needs to be developed.

Example:
You say: "Given all that, I imagine your must feel frustrated, sad, lonely and tired. Are those your feelings?"

He says: "Yes, Dad, I have felt so lonely, so angry with you and mom, and so very frustrated. It has been so painful trying to be your son and pretending to be something I'm not. I'm very hurt and very tired of all this, and I just need your love and acceptance. That would mean the world to me, Dad. Please just love me for who I am."

You say: "Thank you, Son. I heard that you have felt so lonely, angry and frustrated with mom and me. And that it's been so painful pretending to be something you're not. And you're very hurt and tired from this. And all you really want and need is for us to love you just the way you are. Is that it, Son?"

He says: "Yes, Dad. Thank you."

Be aware of your body language. Consciously make sure you are "open" to hear the speaker (do not fold your arms). Show interest in what he is saying. Try not to use a different tone from your child's. If you use a sarcastic tone, that will invalidate him and thwart your efforts to be closer. If you have an angry edge in your voice, your loved one will immediately become defensive. Remember, you do not need to agree—just listen in order to understand. Reflective listening takes a lot of practice and patience. This simple communication skill will help you to see life from his point of view. Above all else, keep breathing!

Be an Effective Communicator

Effective communication also involves the way you share *your* thoughts, feelings and desires without blaming or dictating. This helps the listener to receive your message. If you use "you" statements rather than "I" statements, the listener will become defensive and shut down.

1. Practical tools for effective sharing.

a. Eye contact. Again establish good eye contact. Make sure you are looking into each other's eyes and not down at the floor or somewhere else in the room.

b. Physical touch. Create a conduit between the two of you by using some form of healthy touch. Hold your child's hand(s), place your hand(s) on her shoulder(s) or hug when sharing something important. This will help her receive your message more deeply. Physical touch acts as a conduit of connection and creates greater intimacy between the speaker and listener.

c. Responsible language. Take ownership of your thoughts, feelings and desires by using "I" statements, not "you" statements.

Example 1:
Harmful approach: "You shouldn't believe that people are born gay. You're not really 'gay.' You've been brainwashed into believing such nonsense."

Better approach: "As I'm sure you know by now, I don't believe that people are born gay."

Example 2:

Harmful approach: "You should know the truth that you are going against God's will. You should feel ashamed for wanting to live that way."

Better approach: "I don't believe that God created you with SSA."

The above examples of "you" statements *blame* and *shame* the child and will only strain the relationship further. Your goal is to create open communication so that the power of love can heal. Remember, you cannot control or change anyone. Looking in her eyes, holding her hands and using "I" statements will greatly help your child to feel your sincere heart. And this will help you bring about the secure attachment you are seeking to achieve.

2. Techniques for conflict resolution. Here are healthy tips on how to express yourself when you are hurt and upset by your child's (or others') words or behavior:

a. Data. Name her words or behavior concerning the specific event in question. Do not generalize or speak about the past (for example, "You *always* . . ." or "Last year you . . ."). It's best to avoid using *always* and *never* when you are upset. If you think about it, these are words that children use when they are upset. Do not say, "You always walk away from me when I try to talk to you." Say instead, "When I was talking with you, you walked away from me."

b. Feelings. Use single words to identify your feelings (for example, *sad, mad, glad, afraid, hurt* and so forth). Example: "When I was talking to you and you walked away, I felt hurt."

c. Thoughts. Simply state your opinions, judgments or beliefs, in other words, how you interpreted the data. Example: "My opinion about your walking away while I was talking to you is that I am afraid you don't care about me, that my thoughts and ideas don't matter to you. It reminds me of times when my own father would do that, and that's why it hurts me so much." Take ownership of your reactions rather than blaming the other person. It makes you more powerful, rather than a powerless "victim."

d. *Needs.* Describe clearly what you need. Make your request specific and measurable. Example: "My request is that when I'm talking to you, even if you disagree, please listen and hear me out until I'm finished. I would really appreciate that." Do not make broad, sweeping requests. The more simple, specific and measurable your requests, the better your chances are of getting what you want and need.

e. *Giving.* Express what you are willing to offer. Example: "If you're hurt or offended by what I say, just let me know. I'm more than willing to listen to what you have to say." This creates an exchange of ideas and demonstrates your desire to make the relationship work.

Please don't preach or sermonize while sharing your thoughts and opinions. If you give in to this temptation, you may lose the love connection between you and your child. Remember, your *goal* is to create secure attachment with your child, and your *method* is to do so through responsible communication.

3. Strategies to promote bonding through affirmations. Encourage your child by speaking loving words of affirmation about her character and behavior, and help strengthen weak areas. Examples: "I'm so proud that you are my daughter." "You are very feminine." "I really admire your ability to paint." "I love you just as you are." "You are my beautiful daughter."

Make sure your words are natural and sincere, not forced or manipulative. Everyone wants to be appreciated and affirmed. The more you offer authentic words of affirmation, the more quickly you will find your way back into your child's soul. Affirmations soften the heart.

Practice, Practice and Practice

Effective communication is first a science that is learned by utilizing these basic skills. Then, after much practice, it becomes an art. This will happen when you take the time necessary to develop effective tools for listening and sharing. The more you listen and share, the closer you and your loved one will become. Yes, no doubt you will make mistakes along the way. But we all learn through mistakes, which is why practice is so important.

It is wise to use these communication skills with everyone in your inner circle—your spouse, parents, children, friends and colleagues. These skills are helpful in establishing greater intimacy in all relationships. Practicing good communication is quite similar to weight training. If you regularly lift weights and get in good shape, when you unexpectedly have to carry something heavy, you've got the necessary strength to do it. Accordingly, if you diligently practice communication skills, when tension or conflict arises with your child, you will be more capable of creating intimacy through reflective listening and responsibly sharing your thoughts, feelings and needs.

Trust is a vital part of every relationship, and trust in communication is earned by listening to the other person without judgment. The skills we have been discussing are most beneficial in creating a nonjudgmental place to share. Your child may challenge you to see if you really love her. Take a few deep breaths before you say anything. Your response will have to be *counterintuitive,* going against your gut instinct. Do not lash out. Do not fight back. Bite your tongue, breathe and do some good reflective listening. Most often her questions, comments and challenges are *not* what they appear to be. What you're really dealing with is the pervasive underlying question: *Do you really love me?*

To improve your communications skills, you will have to set aside your disappointment that your child has adopted a "gay" identity (if he has done so). Please try to keep this in mind at all times: people with SSA cannot distinguish between their "gay" identity and just being a person. They do not understand that SSA is the result of wounds and unmet love needs. In their mind, they *are* "gay." And if you do not accept them as "gay" or "lesbian," in their view you do not love them. It does not compute that you could love them but not their homosexuality.

As you seek to deepen the bond between yourself and your son or daughter, be careful and prayerful when choosing your words. Words are very powerful to people with SSA because they are generally very sensitive. Take a deep breath, think first, then put your reflective listening skills to work. And if you feel you are losing ground and heading into a heated argument, when all else fails, just listen and be Mr. and Mrs. KYMS (Keep Your Mouth Shut)!

It bears repeating: a major goal of this treatment plan is not to stop homosexual behavior but to understand how and why those feelings developed in the first place. SSA is an attempt to meet developmental and emotional needs. The key to healing is to lessen SSA's hold on your child while increasing his ability to openly share his feelings, thoughts and needs.

STEP SIX
Make Things Right Between
You and Your SSA Child

In this chapter I will offer suggestions about how to gain welcome entry into the heart and soul of your SSA loved one. This may seem nearly impossible to you today, but believe me, it is not. As you read the stories of success in this chapter, you will discover that constructing a whole new relationship with your child can happen if you persevere.

Of course every person's timetable is unique, because healing depends on temperament, the severity of the wounds and the amount of time you and others are able to invest. What you cannot do, God can, so leave the rest to him.

Express Regrets

I know that by now you've written an inventory of the mistakes you have made in the past based on the causal factors of SSA. Now you may prepare to share your regrets with your SSA child. To help with this, please consult the list of issues you wrote down for the guilt exercise in step one. Create a safe and sacred time to discuss with your son or daughter your own faults and to ask forgiveness for each incident or series of behaviors.

What will you say? How will you find the words? Parents often worry about speaking the right thing at the right time. Truthfully the script couldn't be simpler: "I am very sorry for _____ [name the specific behaviors or words that you feel bad about]. Would you please forgive me?"

Don't be surprised or discouraged if your child tries to brush off your

first efforts, as if the offense had no impact on his life. This is a natural
defense. He may respond by saying, "Yes, I forgive you," or "No, I don't
forgive you," or "That's okay. You were a great dad," or "Don't worry
about it, Dad. That's in the past."

Respond with a key question: "How did my words or actions make you
feel?" You may need to repeat this question many times during this process: "How did it make you feel?" "How did it make you feel?" Keep repeating this until you get an emotionally authentic response. A wonderful
example of the efficacy of repetition is in the film *Good Will Hunting*. The
therapist says to Will, "It's not your fault. It's not your fault. It's not your
fault." Finally, after hearing these words, Will opens his heart and grieves.

After your child begins to share, once again become Mr. or Mrs.
KYMS (Keep Your Mouth Shut) and keep repeating the magic words:
"Thank you, [child's name]. Tell me more." Do not attempt, at this point
to explain circumstances (why you were not there, what was going on in
the family at the time, how you were thinking and so forth). Explana-
tions sound like excuses, and offering them may cause your child to
once again shut down emotionally.

Please remember: *Feelings buried alive never die.* SSA is a developmental and detachment disorder. Your child did not bond with you successfully, so your attempts to rationalize and justify what happened will neither change nor heal him. The best you can do now is to listen and
apologize with a sincere heart. Later, after many feelings have been expressed, he may be open to hearing your thoughts about the past. If not,
then KYMS!

As your child shares, she may blame you for things that you had absolutely no idea about. Perhaps you think that those perceptions are totally off base. Do not try to dispute what's being said or defend yourself.
Let her freely share her feelings and thoughts. Just keep repeating the
magic words: "Thank you, [child's name]. Tell me more." And then listen
once again. As she continues to communicate, repeat as necessary:

"Thank you, [child's' name]. Tell me more." This will allow her to access deeper thoughts and feelings and to begin the natural process of healing. Just keep your own thoughts and feelings out of the way and allow your child to express hurt and pain.

It is important to just listen and be, as Dr. Alice Miller calls it, a "sympathetic witness." Feelings are just feelings. They are neither right nor wrong. Your child's perceptions are his perceptions, and the key to healing is grieving. Again, "we must feel and be real in order to heal." We do not need answers, and we do not need someone to make things better or tell us that it did not happen that way or otherwise try to fix us. We just need someone to be with us as a sympathetic witness as we grieve the losses in our past.

During this process, try to prepare yourself to accept your SSA child's anger and remind yourself that anger is a defense for hurt and pain. The more you are able to listen to your child's anger and respond in love, the greater her chances for healing. Even at that, healing may not happen at once. It may require numerous attempts. It has often been said that the process of healing is like peeling an onion: layer after layer has to be removed over a period of time.

As we've seen, those who have adopted the "gay" identity often believe that they were born that way, so they may be unable to hear your apologies or attempts to identify and rectify family dynamics that caused their SSA. Therefore it may involve numerous attempts and much effort to finally get them to a point where they are ready to express their true thoughts and feelings about the past.

That raises an important point: Please do not apologize in the context of healing SSA. Make your apologetic gestures completely independent of the issue of homosexuality. You are simply a parent taking responsibility for past mistakes. Let that be the sole focus of this act of humility and reconciliation.

Bonding and Boundaries

The first two stages of life, which take place within the child's first three years, create the template for all future relationships. Let's take a look at these stages.

Stage one. Stage one, from conception to about one or one and a half years old, is the bonding stage. The most important figure in this stage is the mother. There is a symbiotic connection between mother and child. The child is completely dependent on her for all life functions. Even when the father is involved in the care of the child during stage one, it is the mother-child bonding that establishes secure attachment.

If children experience secure attachment in stage one, they will feel bonded, secure, loved, understood and cared for. Their attitude will be, "I am able to share my feelings, thoughts and desires. I know that people will be there to meet my needs." On the other hand, when children's needs are not met, as noted researcher John Bowlby has observed, they go from protesting (crying to get attention), to despairing (when no one comes to feed, change or hold them), to detaching (I cannot trust anyone to meet my needs, so I will just shut up or act cute or act out). This lays the groundwork for future attachment issues.

Stage two. In stage two, from one and a half until three years of age, the child begins to crawl, walk and then talk—the terrific twos! Here children learn appropriate boundaries while gaining affirmation for moving away and discovering their own identity. We call this stage a time of separation, individuation and differentiation. They are learning to say, in so many words, "I'm not you." This is the main reason the operative word during this phase of development is *no*. "No!" means "I want to discover things for myself." Children at this age are establishing themselves as distinctly different entities from mom and dad.

If children receive encouragement for moving away and exploring, and simultaneously learn to receive healthy limits and proper boundaries so they do not hurt themselves, they will feel affirmed and will learn the art of self-regulation. When stage two is successfully completed, the child will feel powerful, valuable, competent and worthy.

In the case of many SSA men, they were "good boys," more gentle and compliant than typical males. They did not give their mothers, in particular, any trouble. But that is not healthy, because boys are by nature more aggressive than girls and therefore often make trouble. Be careful of the good little boy who feels your feelings and tries to please you, rather than being who he is and discovering his own masculinity. If you see this happening in your son or grandson, encourage him to express his feelings and not be a caretaker for the parent.[1] Some girls may be more aggressive, loud and strong. If affirmed by dad and mom, their innate heterosexuality will blossom. If criticized or rejected, this may endanger their sense of gender identity.

It is very important for dad to be involved in stage two of his son's life. The girl will continue to gender-identify with mom. ("We are both girls. I am like you. You are like me.") However, the boy soon discovers that he and mom aren't quite alike. ("You are different from me. I am different from you.") His father, or a male role model, must then bring him into the world of the masculine. Now he sees, "I am like you, Daddy. We are similar." If the father is *not* available, either physically or emotionally, the son will miss this important stage of gender identification. This missed gender identification developmental stage lays the foundation for future SSA in boys.

Girls need secure attachment with their mothers during this stage. If the daughter is more aggressive than her mother or her nature is contrary to that of her mom, this may create a barrier to bonding. If the daughter withdraws, this may also disrupt healthy mother-daughter attachment. The mother needs to join in her daughter's world, thus establishing a healthy female alliance. A girl needs to view her mother as a safe

---

[1]Read Joseph and Linda Ames Nicolosi's *A Parent's Guide to Preventing Homosexuality* (Downers Grove, Ill.: InterVarsity Press, 2002), for more details.

and healthy role model of femininity. She then wants to grow up to be like her mom.

We've seen how Bonnie and Adrian's SSA developed. SSA starts very early. That is why many will say, "Since I was a child, I had SSA." The core wounding likely occurred in the earliest stages of development.

It hurts to expose and explore old wounds. As you seek to bond with your child, you may find yourself crying with him. Be assured that when you show your feelings, chances are your child will show his, because those with SSA tend to be sensitive kids. In the process of healing, that works in your favor. Sensitive kids may get in touch with their feelings more easily than other children; however, because these kids are not securely attached, focus on establishing an alliance of intimacy and sharing before you establish too many rules and boundaries. *Please remember: Bonding is necessary before boundaries.*

On the other hand, your child may need firm boundaries and discipline if she is unruly and out of control. Why establish boundaries at this late date? So your child will not take advantage of you and others. Furthermore, this will help her learn the necessary skills of self-regulation, not throwing tantrums or trying to manipulate you or other people. You need to maintain the parental position and never abdicate to her. If you allow her to get her way when acting childish, this is not love, and it is a formula for failure. However, if the child is compliant and disciplined, "the good child," focus on bonding. You will need to experiment. There are no hard-and-fast rules that fit every child in every situation. Much will depend on age, temperament, character and your child's needs.

The primary emotions are love, anger, fear and sadness. Anger is used to protect the wounded heart, so when your child gets angry during this healing process, it is good. Accept his anger, reminding yourself that underneath all anger is a hurt and wounded child. If you are afraid of anger, this will be difficult for you. However, if you can quiet yourself and simply listen and give him time, he will move through the anger and into the pain. Again, use the magic words: "Thank you, [child's name]. Please tell me more."

Join your child in her emotions and do not resist. Paraphrase what was shared. Listen with your heart and not your head. Do not lash out and try to correct your child's misperceptions. Remember, this is about your child and not about you. No matter how young or old your child is, she will always regard you as dad and mom and always need your love. Say, "I love you, and home will always be a safe place for you." Eventually, once she releases her pain, she will be open to receiving your love.

Ask About Your Child's History of SSA

While you are working hard at bonding with your child, it is important for you to find out about his SSA. But how do you approach the subject? Here are four questions I suggest the same-sex parent ask the SSA child. Both parents may be present for these discussions. However, the same-sex parent should lead.

1. When did you begin to experience same-sex attractions?

2. Has this made life difficult for you? Have you ever been ridiculed at school, church or synagogue?

3. What type of men/women are you attracted to (age, body type, personality and other attributes)?

4. What would you like from me/us?

Use good listening skills when your child answers these questions. Do not interrupt, comment or correct. Again, speak those magic words: "Thank you. Tell me more." Learn about your child's journey. After he has finished sharing, it is your turn to reciprocate. It is most important for you to express your feelings about his lonely and painful journey; about how sad it makes you feel that you never knew what he was going through. "I am so sorry for all the pain and loneliness that you have experienced. My heart breaks for you. Please feel free to open up and share. I want to know all of you."

It is important to understand what type of person your child is attracted to, because it will tell you a lot about her SSA. For example, if your daughter is attracted to older women, most likely she has a homo-emotional wound and is looking for a mother's love in the arms of older women. If she's attracted to someone her own age, she may have a homo-social wound, in which case she is looking for acceptance by her same-sex peers. Men with SSA are also attracted to older, same-age or younger males. This represents homo-emotional and/or homo-social wounding as well. Men and women with SSA may also have what author and healer Leanne Payne calls a "cannibal compulsion," because they seek to absorb from another person that which they lack within themselves. Referring to one of her clients, Payne writes, "He was looking at the other young man and loving a lost part of himself, a part that he could not recognize and accept."[2]

Generally speaking, many SSA sons did not experience being affirmed by their fathers and same-sex peers, so they failed to internalize a strong sense of their gender identity. The same is true of an SSA girl and her mother and same-sex peers. Now, as adolescents or adults, these people are looking for that acceptance in the arms of another person. You may think your son seems strong and masculine, so why would he look for that in someone else, especially in a man who may appear to be similar to him? It is because he does not experience the strength of his own gender identity and instead is seeking that affirmation by joining with another man. Remember, it is *gender identity confusion*. He may have been detached from Dad and his peers, so he never internalized his own sense of being a boy and fitting in with the other guys. Now he is pursuing that lost sense of masculinity through other men. After puberty, those basic needs for bonding became eroticized.

---

[2]Leanne Payne, *The Healing of the Homosexual* (Westchester, Ill.: Crossway, 1985), pp. 2-5.

If he is attracted to young men or boys, most often he is trying to heal wounds that occurred at that age. I once counseled a policeman who was strong, handsome, educated—every woman's dream. He was attracted to thirteen-year-old boys, however, because that is when his major wounding occurred. He is unconsciously drawn to young boys attempting to heal unresolved issues from that period in his life. Of course, that does not work.

Several teenagers I have counseled have fantasized about having sex with strong, powerful, loving men. Their own dads were very loving, just not assertive. The sons wanted their fathers to be more powerful, more "in charge" of the family. They hungered for a strong father figure, and that hunger became sexualized during adolescence.

Some men are attracted to effeminate males, just as some women are attracted to masculine females. This may indicate an opposite-sex wound: men fearing intimacy with women, and women fearing intimacy with men. They seek refuge in the arms of someone of the same gender who poses no threat. Meanwhile the effeminate men and masculine women are dis-identified with their own gender. They seek to fulfill what was never developed by joining with someone who epitomizes a strong male or healthy female. Deep within, they long to become that to which they are drawn.

By knowing the type of person to which your child is attracted, you can begin to understand and identify her wounds and, step-by-step, help meet her needs. Again, expect rejection. This is a battle of love. She is wounded, hurt and angry. You must win her back. It is either going to be you or the girlfriend. Your love will last. The partner's, according to statistics about homosexual relationships, will not.[3]

Ask your child what kind of support from you would be most helpful.

---

[3]According to a study in David McWhirter and Andrew Mattison's *The Male Couple* (Prentice-Hall, 1984), of 156 same-sex male relationships lasting one to thirty-seven years, only 7 couples (5 percent) together less than five years maintained sexual fidelity. The other 95 percent of couples were all having sex outside of the relationship, which means 100 percent sexual infidelity after being together five or more years.

If he has adopted a "gay" identity, he will want your approval. It is important to state, "I love and accept you just as you are." You may use these words verbatim. *This does not mean you approve of your child's lifestyle*. It does mean that you accept him unconditionally, right now. Change is not necessary for him to be loved and accepted by you. Love is the medicine that heals all pain. And whatever his beliefs may be, underneath is a wounded heart needing acceptance and love. Focus on the heart, and the mind will follow.

Meet Unmet Needs for Love

Without your love and acceptance, the SSAD community becomes your child's only haven in which to feel loved and understood. That is why it is so important for you to create an environment of acceptance in your home and spiritual community. You may not be able to empathize, but you sure can sympathize. Apologize for not being there when you were needed the most. Listen. Promise you will be there from now on—but only if you are willing to make that commitment. Avoid making false promises. You will break your child's heart once again if you do. Remember, these are often hypersensitive people—one reason why they developed SSA. As Dr. Jeffrey Satinover has observed, they may be more prone to anxiety because of this hypersensitivity.[4]

Too often, fathers' and sons' characters (as well as mothers' and daughters') are mismatched. So often we see a sensitive son and an aggressive or emotionally unavailable father. It is like a round peg in a square hole; they do not fit and cannot understand each other. I counseled a family in which the son was an artist and the father was a minister heavily into sports. The son could easily share his thoughts and feeling with his mother, as he had done for most of his life. She understood him perfectly. But there was no

---

[4]Jeffrey Satinover, *Homosexuality and the Politics of Truth* (Grand Rapids: Baker Books, 1996), p. 222.

connection between the son and his dad. There was no bonding between the son and his same-sex peers. In fact, he had been teased and mocked for most of his life for being an artist. He felt more comfortable with his mom and other girls at school. This was unhealthy for proper male development and a perfect scenario for SSA development.

Your Child Is Not Responsible for Your Well-Being

Another unhealthy dynamic is for your SSA child to feel responsible for your happiness. She may have seen, perceived or experienced your pain while growing up. These sensitive kids take it to the extreme, believing that it is their responsibility to make everything okay for you. This becomes a lifetime pattern of pleasing. You may or may not be aware of this in her. Therefore it will be very important to ask, "Do you feel responsible for my well-being?" "Do you think you have to take care of me?" Listen carefully to the response. If she says "yes" in any way, then state clearly, "It is *not* your responsibility to take care of me."

After teaching this lesson in one of my Parent's Teleconferencing Classes, a mother went to her twenty-five-year-old son and asked that question. She received a definite yes from him. She then told him, "You are not responsible for my well-being. I can take care of myself, and Dad will take care of me too."

The son was shocked. "Really? Do you mean that? I want you to write it down and sign it!"

Well, she did better than that. She created a certificate stating that her son was no longer responsible for her well-being from that date forth. She signed, dated and laminated it. He was so delighted that he framed it and put it on his wall! Other parents have repeated these words of liberation to their SSA kids with similar positive results.

What to Expect As Your Child Heals and Grows

Several parents have asked me to explain what their child is going through while in therapy for healing unwanted SSA. Some of their children's requests and behaviors have been off-putting to dad and mom. Here are potential phases that your SSA child may go through while in therapy or simply reprocessing through developmental stages of childhood, adolescence and adulthood. People do not pass through these phases exactly in this order but experience the following stages as they seek to accomplish specific developmental tasks. Your child will . . .

1. *Set new boundaries with you.* He will probably not want you to know about many things he is going through. Finally separating and individuating from you, perhaps for the first time, he is emotionally reprocessing through stage two of life (developmentally one and a half to three years of age), learning to stand on his own feet, differentiating from you. He most likely will request "space," not wanting to share much so that he might experience thoughts and feelings independent of you.[5]

2. *Establish a new set of rules for relating.* Your SSA child needs to know that it is safe to express needs and that he will be respected, not treated like a child or punished. He is learning to become more in tune and in touch with feelings and to express those feelings and thoughts as a responsible adult.

3. *Seek to be accepted as your child is in this moment (SSA and all).* He needs to know that you love him and that there's no need to "change" to be acceptable in your eyes. He needs you to listen without judgment. You may not agree with many of his choices, but they are your child's, and all people need to learn life's lessons on their own. Then he will come into personal power, standing as a more mature adult. During this phase he

---

[5]Be careful with teenagers who have been emotionally detached from their parents most of their lives. In this case, they will need to experience healthy bonding with both mom and dad.

may be acting out in ways you think unnecessary, or relating to people you deem inappropriate influences. However, he needs to work through this on his terms. People in therapy to heal from unwanted SSA often surround themselves with healthy same-sex friends.

4. *Eventually enroll you in the healing process, wanting to resolve past issues.* Or you may enroll your child into your healing process, inviting him to attend family healing sessions or healing seminars. After you pass the test of the previous phases (that is, listening without judgment, allowing decision making, agreeing to newfound independence) then he begins to feel more comfortable communicating about issues from the past.

5. *Begin to share about deeper hurts and wounds, perhaps even blaming you for all kinds of things you never knew he thought and felt.* Now you employ, as you have been doing all along, the good listening skills you have learned. The more your child grieves, the healthier he will become, and the less he will need SSA and related behaviors.

6. *Develop healthy relationships with the same-gender parent, siblings, relatives and peers.* As your child experiences healthy same-sex bonding, he will begin to internalize a strong sense of his own gender identity. Often, then, opposite-sex desires will emerge.

As your child works through these phases of healing and growth, you may sometimes feel hurt and confused. Please know that this is a new season in both your life and that of your child. Please be patient. During such times, people with SSA learn more about themselves, learning to define thoughts, feelings and needs. Your child must work through these stages of growth, often independent of you, in order to claim his own gender identity.

Make an Affirmation Recording for Your Child

Many times our children did not hear enough words of encouragement while growing up. They carry deep psychic wounds in their hearts— messages of criticism and judgment. For this reason, if you are the same-sex parent, you may want to consider making an affirmation tape or CD for your SSA child to help heal a sense of low self-worth.

Mom, make an affirmation recording for your daughter. Dad, make an affirmation recording for your son. Below are five suggestions of what to include. They are followed by sample affirmations written by some of my clients, whom I asked to make a list of things they wish their parents or friends had said or done while they were growing up. Both lists will give you clues about what your child needs. Or you may want to ask him what he would like you to share on the tape or CD.

- Speak about his being, who he is as a man. "You are my precious son. I am proud of you. I believe in you. I admire your strength of character. You are strong and powerful. I love you just as you are. I love you."

- Speak about aspects of her behavior, things that you admire and want to encourage. "I think you are a great public speaker. I believe you can accomplish whatever you set your mind to. You make me smile with your humorous stories and jokes. You are an amazing athlete and singer." Use many adjectives to describe your child. The more powerful and believable your language is, the deeper the impact will be on her psyche.

- Genuinely praise his manliness or her femininity. "You are quite a handsome man." "You are very masculine and powerful." "I am proud that you are my son." "I see you inner strength and it's awesome." Use specific characteristics of manliness or femininity that apply to your son or daughter.

- Speak words of blessing for her life, "My wish is for you to fulfill the purpose of your life, to pursue your destiny and live it to its fullest. You are a daughter of God. I know he will always watch over you. I pray that you may experience God's love and our love each moment of your life. I will always be there for you, no matter what. I give you my blessing." Use these magic words as well: "I believe in you." Say them over and over again on the recording and in your daily life.

- Use beautiful music in the background. This will help the message go deeper into both your child's conscious and unconscious minds.

The recording may last five minutes or longer. It is not the length that is important. It is the love behind the message that will reach into your child's heart and soul. Let him feel your love through your spoken words. You might want to make a tape or CD for each of your children so your SSA child does not feel singled out. You might give the recording as a gift for a special event or holiday. Some parents made a CD for each of their children and gave it to them for Christmas or Hanukkah. The purpose is to instill a deep sense of belonging and connection between you and your child. It will be a cherished gift.

David: Positive things I wish my father had said:

- I love you, Son.
- I'm proud to be your father.
- David, you are tall and handsome.
- I love you, Son, and I give you my blessing.
- You are strong, brave and courageous.
- You exceed my expectations as a son.
- I want to spend time with you.
- David, I appreciate you.
- You are very important to me.
- You are very talented, my son.
- David, you are worthy to be loved.

David: Positive things I wish my peers would say and do:

- David, we are your friends, and you are dear to us.
- You are strong and handsome.
- We accept you.
- We look up to you.
- We want to hang out with you.
- You deserve the best.
- We enjoy being around you.
- We appreciate you.
- I'd pick you first to be on my team.
- We love you, David.
- I would like to be buddies with you.

John's affirmations desired from his dad:

- I love you, John.
- I respect who you are.
- I am proud that you are my son.
- I care about what you think and feel.
- John, you are very important to me.
- I want to spend time with you.
- You are a man just like me.
- I want to hug you.
- You belong to me.
- I am proud of you.
- John, you are unique, and I love you.
- John, here is the way men walk.
- John, I want you to have the best in life.
- John, I am with you all the way.

John's affirmations desired from friends:

- John, you belong.
- You make a difference.
- You are one of us.
- You are courageous.
- You are cool.
- We need you.
- We are here for you, man.

Eric: Things I wish my Dad had said to me:

- How wonderful that I have been given a third son to enjoy and to cherish like no other man ever could. What other man has the privilege of calling you son?

- I am so proud of the unique and gifted young man you are.

- Your body is masculine. Your face is masculine. Your mannerisms are masculine. Your voice is masculine. You are tall and handsome, like all the men in our family.

- I accept your creativity and sensitivity as God-given manly traits. Even though I was not allowed or encouraged to share my feelings while growing up, I recognize that you must do this to be true to yourself. I admire the level to which you feel things and the way you express them. I love it when you share from your heart. This is how I learn about you!

- You are strong, powerful and manly, like me. You are a natural leader.

- You measure up in every possible way to my expectations for you. You are intelligent, artistic, athletic and thoughtful.

- I will take the time necessary to teach you how to live in the world of men. This includes sports, business and how to relate to women.

- You come from a line of great men and fall right into place.

- You are constantly in my heart.

- You are masculine and athletic.

- I will take the time to know you and to relate to you in the unique way that you need. You can trust me, for I am on your side.

Eric: Things I wish peers had said to me:
Younger years:

- Do you want to come over to my house and play?

- Can you make it to my birthday party? You would add something really special just by being there.

- Hey, a bunch of us are getting together to play some ball. Can you make it over to the field?

High school and college years:

- Anyone would be lucky to have you as a friend.

- Wow, you are really talented. I admire your architectural drawings and your ability to act and sing onstage. Man, that takes guts.

- I think you're so cool.

- You are really a great guy. I've heard other guys say they think you're cool.

- It would be awesome if we could spend some time together, just hanging out, you know? Just a few of us guys?

- Hey, a bunch of us are going skiing for the weekend. Would you like to come with us?

- Man—how did you get so talented? Will you show me how to draw, write, act or sing like that?

- Wow, you're a strong guy; you must work out.

Write a Letter to Your Son or Daughter

By putting your thoughts and feelings in writing, you give your child the opportunity to better understand you. It also allows you to gain insights into yourself. The letter should include the following four aspects:

1. *Regrets.* Talk about things you said or did that you feel sorry about, for example, not spending time together while she was growing up, speaking to her in a hurtful way, treating her disrespectfully, leaving the parenting responsibility to your spouse and not being involved, criticizing and complaining about her and so forth.

2. *Repentance.* Apologize. Ask forgiveness for the things you did

wrong, for harsh words you spoke and for lack of involvement. For example, "Please forgive me for leaving you alone so many times in your life. I am sorry." "Please forgive me for not listening to you and just letting your mother take care of you." "Please forgive me for not telling you what a wonderful young man you are. It's hard for me to express my feelings openly." Tell him that you want to know how your actions affected him; ask him how he felt then and how he feels now. Getting his emotional feedback is very important.

3. *Reconciliation.* Write about what you would like to do now to make amends for past mistakes. For example, "I would like to spend more time with you, going on fishing trips, sharing with you more regularly, attending your theater productions and becoming more involved in your life."

4. *Restoration.* As the parent, offer your blessing on your child's life. Write your wishes and dreams for her based on her innate talents and dreams. "I believe you will have a wonderful life. I give you my blessing. You are a wonderful child of God, and I know you will fulfill your destiny." (See step three for references to books on offering "The Blessing" to your child.)

You may need to write several versions of your letter before actually giving one to your child. You may find yourself venting at first: Release your anger, pain, disgust, confusion and bitterness. Express what you really think about his same-sex attractions. It is important for you to let out all your feelings in Technicolor! Then be sure to destroy these drafts of the letter.

The final version will have less of your gut reactions and more of you taking personal responsibility for any mistakes you have made, asking for forgiveness, sharing about the kind of relationship you wish to create now and then offering your love and blessing. Share the final letter with your spouse or a close friend before giving it to your child. Get some feedback from an objective source.

Some children welcome recordings and letters with open arms. Other times they reject them, believing such efforts to be ploys, intended to make them change. Again, be persistent. Let your child know that your intention is simply to express your love, regrets and desires for his or her life. Be patient and persistent, and don't accept no as an answer.

Example of a Dad's and a Mom's Letter to a Son

Dear Rob,

When I think of you, I see so many great things. I see a person who has a great sense of humor and very sharp wit. I have no doubt that comes from my side of the family! You have so many other tremendous talents:

You are able to think outside of the box and see things in a different way.

You have amazing insight and knowledge of so many things: cars, real estate, weather, music, movies and, most important of all, people (having very good insight about people and their feelings and what they are going through).

This knowledge is coupled with your great ability to remember things. Whether it's lyrics to a song, features and specifications about cars, or layouts of home floor plans, you simply amaze me with your ability to accurately recall all these things.

You are very strong in your personal characteristics and very protective of those you care for. You did not give in to temptation on drugs in school, even though they were everywhere and easily accessible.

One of your greatest gifts is your great capacity for empathy, concern and love for others that is backed up by action. You "walk the walk."

You have so many gifts, but I believe you sell yourself short. I wanted to tell you these things because I don't think I have told you enough, at least to the point where you see and believe these things yourself.

When I think of you, I also think of areas where I wish I had been different with you. I worked hard to provide for our family. There is nothing wrong with working hard and being a good provider; however, I realize now that I should have been more balanced in my time with you. Knowing some of the things I have learned recently, I realize that I should have continued to pursue you and your love no matter how difficult you made it, no matter how many times you pushed me away. Little did I realize then how important it was to have that special time with you . . . one on one. Those moments of you pushing me away, I believe now, were really calls from you, asking me to pull you back into my life . . . but I had to pursue you, and I know now that I did not try hard enough.

I'm not exactly sure what drove the wedge in our relationship during that time. I don't believe it was any one thing, but a culmination of numerous small things that painted a picture that made you feel you were not important to me. Nothing could be further from the truth.

In many ways we are a lot alike, especially when it comes to communicating what's going on inside our hearts, especially when there is pain involved. This is an area where I have struggled throughout my life, and I am still learning. I know that I need to go beyond myself and share what I'm feeling instead of keeping it bottled up inside, where resentment and anger grow and fester. This lack of sharing has created self-imposed barriers that hurt people I care very much about.

I know this happened quite often with your mom and me, especially after you and Mark were born. Many times I felt like an outsider as mom would be doing the things she needed to do for you and Mark as a mom. She was doing a great job of being a mom but, I thought, not as great of a job when it came to being a wife. I had difficulty in sharing mom with you and Mark, and often felt resentful at the lack of time I had with her due to the time she spent with you and your brother. I would retreat inside myself and lick my wounds and pull back from her and the rest of the family. My thoughts were that if this person really loved me, she would know what I was feeling and that I was hurting. She would pursue me and ask me what was wrong and not stop until everything was better. There was one big problem: when your mom did those things, I did not share with her what I was feeling. She knew there was something wrong, but I wouldn't express it. It was too late, and the damage was already done. So I would keep holding back and not communicating, almost as if to punish or hurt her for the pain I felt. I can still feel the pain, even as I write now. The feeling of being left out, of being ignored and not wanted, cut through my heart like a knife.

In reality mom did nothing wrong. She was trying to balance being a great mom and a great wife, and she was both. Most of my pain was self-induced because I continually failed to let her in and to share my pain and suffering with her. What was worse is when we finally did have time together it was marred by my inability to let go of my past hurts and pains. The barrier stood tall and strong, and nothing was allowed to venture forth or to return back to my heart, and I lost so many opportunities to get the affection and love I so very much wanted and needed. For the most part, I really had no one to blame but myself, and it became a vicious cycle.

I finally started doing what I should have been doing a lot earlier. I started opening up and sharing my thoughts, hurts and feelings about our relationship. By communicating these things with your mom, I realized how much your mother loved me and how frustrated she also was that we had less time together. I experienced the depth of her caring for me in ways I had never known before. I wish I had talked to her so much earlier, so that the pain and hurt would not have lasted so long, but those were my decisions. I became so much more secure in her love, so even when those situations still arose and we couldn't spend time together, the stinging hurt was gone because I was so much more secure in her love. This is where I believe I may have failed with you.

I have always had such a deep love for you and will continue to until my last breath. Where I have fallen short has been in my ability to let you know this in no uncertain terms. I feel that there have been ways that I have let you down, that there were things I needed to do to make you feel secure in my love for you.

Somewhere in our lives you have needed emotional support from me in different areas; somehow I didn't know exactly what those needs were or did not know how to give you what you needed. It is not that I didn't want to, but I didn't know how to, or that I needed to. I thought you always knew how much I cared for you. I know there were many times when I tried to get special time with just you when you were small. I remember just the two of us playing catch or soccer on the front lawn. Invariably, many times Mark would see us and join in and kind of dominate our activity, which left you on the outside, not being able to compete at the level of your older brother. Knowing what I have learned recently, I wish that I had been more careful and had picked better times for us, times when Mark was playing with his friends or was out with mom so that we could have more time together, just the two of us.

Little did I realize how very important having that time with you was and how much you needed me to do that for you and with you. Over time apparently those times of hurt and pain because of not receiving the special time you needed with me got to be too much. I believe it became too painful for you to pursue something you thought you might never attain, so you understandably stopped trying.

I believe that these past hurts have added up and created an environment where you pulled back from me. I believe you felt about me as I did in the past about your mom, that if I really loved you I would know what you were feeling and know that you were hurting. If I really loved you, I would keep coming after you, no matter how many times you pushed me away. I believe you have held onto those hurts and pains, which has built a safe wall that has kept us from enjoying those special times when it was just you and me.

My hope and wish is that someday we can talk, so that I can better understand what you have needed and still need from me. I also hope that you will forgive me for not being there for you in the past, in the ways that you needed me. All I hope for is just another chance for you to open your heart to me, so that I can give you the love and affection I have for you. I am so proud of you and the great qualities you have as a person and as my son.

My last hope is that one day you will get an answer to the special prayer from God. Not that this trial be removed, but dear God, please grant me your wisdom to help me understand your plan for me in this life, with this cross that you've asked me to bear. Please grant me your grace, courage and strength to carry this cross, so that from this cross I may be a blessing to others.

I believe that God will answer that special prayer. Your life will be an example of healing and love and what others can have if they are open to healing also.

With all my love,

Dad

Dear Rob,

Oh how I love you. You brighten up my life in a way few others can. You bring joy and humor wherever you go. Everyone loves you, Rob. You make us smile. I know you have heard that many times over. Please believe it. Dad and I try to give you our unconditional love. Beyond that, you have earned the love from those in your life by the person you are. I am so proud of you.

How happy Dad and I were when you were born to us! I prayed for two boys, and you made that dream a reality. When I had trouble late in my pregnancy, and you struggled through a very difficult birth, you fought so hard to survive. And when you were ten days old and we nearly lost you to a crib death, again you fought against the odds. It was not easy for you from the beginning, but you overcame the adversity you were challenged with. As long as you had your Matchbox cars with you, you seemed happy just being.

You are so easy to be with. You have filled my life with love and laughter. I remember how brave you were when you got off the ride at Disney World and told us your heart was racing so fast. Later when we found out you had a heart problem and needed an ablation, you taught me how to be brave. I was so frightened, and again you were so brave. You have a rare inner strength. I admire your will and determination. Sometimes we call it "stubborn." Hmmm.

You are such an interesting person. Quiet in nature, you have many talents and attributes that make you the special person that you are—your artistic talent, your creative ability to see things differently, a flair for design and architecture that you freely share with us. Your breadth of knowledge of cars still amazes me. Who knew when you picked up that first Motor Trend magazine when you were seven that you would make your knowledge of cars your trademark! You had a dream and you held onto it. I am proud of you.

I feel sad beyond words when I look back at the turmoil you've experienced in your life. I search my heart and mind trying to understand where I could have made a difference. I loved you the best I knew how, and yet I failed you in a way that you needed me to be there for you. You had special needs that I didn't realize. That breaks my heart. I wish I had been paying better attention to you and made better use of our time together.

You have carried a huge burden from your early teens. I wonder if I had been more in tune with you, your thoughts and your feelings, if I could have helped you to find different answers to your questions and frustrations. I wish I could have saved you from the fear, the heartache and the isolation you experienced. My heart breaks when I realize the times I should have been there for you, but I was not. Although I was physically present, emotionally we did not connect, and I didn't recognize your needs. Although I wish I could change the past, I accept that I cannot.

However, I can be a part of the formation of the future. I want to be here for you today in a way that I have not been over the years. I am listening to you differently now, more cognizant of your pain and the hurt you have endured. My inclination is to try to help you any way I can. I see that same trait in you, so I think you will be able to relate to my feeling. You are always the one others reach out to when they need someone to listen, to care and to be there for them. Better than that, you have a gift for reaching out to them before they even ask you. I missed that opportunity with you. I have learned a lot from you. I still need to learn more about how to interact with you, to meet the needs you have in your life, and to express my love for you in a way that is meaningful to you. My hope is that we can work through the journey ahead together. You hold such a special place in my heart and in my life. I love you today, and I will love you forever.

I love you,

Mom

These parents sat together with their son as they read their letters to him. When they finished, they all shared deeply and cried. It created more trust and bonding between them. Other parents mailed or e-mailed their letters and shared about the contents later on. How you do this is entirely up to you. To determine the best method, just think: Which way will create greater intimacy?

Attend Healing Seminars and Participate in Family Healing Sessions

There are several excellent healing seminar programs available for individual, couple or family healing (see the addendum for more information). These experiential programs are designed to help you and your child resolve personal and relational issues. Many couples attend without their child, gaining tremendous insight from those who struggle with unwanted SSA. This has enabled them more deeply to understand the heart and mind of their child. These extremely powerful and transforming weekends are worth about six months of therapy.

You may also consider participating in family healing sessions. Some therapists are trained in family therapy and may facilitate this experience. I have worked with many families where a loved one is dealing with SSA, and it is astounding to see years of pain and bitterness melt away. During these sessions, each family member has a chance to share his "truth" with the others. Following these moments, the pain subsides and real bonding occurs. Underneath all the hurt, anger and pain is love, understanding and forgiveness.

Following are two stories about family reconciliation. In the first, a father changes his attitude toward his son and radical healing begins. In the second, parents change their perspective about their daughter's SSA, and from that moment their lives take a dramatic turn for the better.

Father-Son Reconciliation

By a mother who attended a support group for parents

I am returning the materials I borrowed in 2001. So much time has passed since then and so much has happened. When I first came, my son was thirteen and his father detested him. Now my son is fifteen, and his father is his biggest fan.

The turning point for me was reading *Coming Out Straight*. I have never read anything sadder than that. I shared the info with my husband, and he started making changes in his attitude. He has taken our son on several trips, played sports with him, talked with him and listened in a nonjudgmental way. *Most of all, he stopped rejecting him*. Now when he looks at our son, it is a look of love, not dissatisfaction. He understands why our son is this way and what can be done to lead him out into the fullness of his person.

You have no idea what kind of difference it makes in our son's behavior. At first, of course, our son rejected his father's affection. Not used to it and in general uncomfortable around males, he did not like being touched and he didn't know how to react. It took us a year of patience, trials and failures until our son started emerging out of his shell. He actually goes to his father to tell him different things, something so simple, yet completely unheard of before. *For the first time in his life he feels comfortable with his father and himself.* At the age of fourteen, our son referred to his father as "my dad" for the first time in his life. Before, he tried calling his father by his first name or referred to him as "mom's husband." For me, that day was more important than the day my son learned to walk. Because in a way this was the day my son took his first step as the person God had created him to be.

A Daughter's Homecoming

By a mom and dad

We found out about Sarah's SSA when she was nineteen years old but didn't discuss it much after that. When she went to college, Sarah told us that she was having an affair with another girl in her youth group from the time she was fourteen. We responded negatively, thinking that homosexuality was worse than murder. We also believed that homosexuality was a choice. We thought she had chosen this herself.

Instead of compassion and sympathy, we responded in judgment. We told her, "You'll go to hell. This is sinful behavior." We had various arguments after that. She moved out and closer to the gay community downtown. She felt much better with them. There she was accepted.

We spent four years in that situation. We helped her out financially, but were at odds about everything else. There was no connection. She revealed to us later that she just wanted us to drive down there, especially mom, and pick her up and take her home. She told us that she had gone through the most brutal experiences of her life while living in the gay community. She said, "Mom and Dad, you threw me to the wolves!" We know that she hasn't told us everything yet. . . . She felt abandoned and left alone by the two people she loved and needed the most. She even contemplated suicide but didn't because she thought it would hurt us too deeply!

She was truly a child looking for love in all the wrong places because we didn't understand her in the ways that she needed at the time. We didn't love her as God loved her. We told her how we wanted her to be and how we needed her to conform to our demands. And it sent her straight into the arms of the sad gay world. We would be friendly one minute, then get angry the next and say things like, "Why are you living this horrible lifestyle?" We were critical of her friends and never socialized with them.

Two and half years ago, we were going to buy a house. The Spirit of God moved us to ask her if she wanted to live with us. She said she would if her girlfriend could live there too. Somehow we agreed. That was the beginning of reestablishing our relationship. But it lacked relational substance. We were still locked into the mindset that this was rebellious and chosen behavior. This produced anger and judgment, and caused us not to connect in the ways that she needed. We continued to neglect her essential needs for love.

Our church was very judgmental about homosexuality. We didn't feel comfortable to speak with anyone about this, so we ended up leaving. We felt alone, in pain and anguish. We quit going to church and tried desperately to find a place where *we* belonged.

A big break came when her girlfriend charged our credit card for thousands of dollars! Our daughter had the strength to throw her out of the house. We asked Sarah to see a counselor who was a friend of ours from church. She finally agreed to see him once and then began having regular sessions.

In late 2004, we said we must do something because we were in deep despair. I (Dad) went to my office one Saturday morning. I found in my desk drawer, among a group of papers, a letter to the editor I had kept for years that mentioned homosexuality. I had this piece of paper for so long it had turned brown! I believe this was divine intervention. In that article it mentioned PFLAG and PFOX. I eventually went to the PFOX website and spoke with Regina Griggs, their national director. She told me about Richard Cohen. That was the beginning of our enlightenment.

Before Christmas of that year, we were going around in circles and getting nowhere. It was hurting our marriage. Our hearts had darkened until we met Richard. Then we participated in the Parent's Teleconferencing Class and attended a Love/Sex/Intimacy (LSI) Healing Seminar. The suffering and pain of the SSA strugglers at that healing seminar opened our eyes. We saw them crying and re-alized that our daughter felt the same way!

During the past eight months, we have progressed more than in the last six years. Last night, our daughter called, saying, "I feel so much pain. Can I come over and share with you?" This would never have happened before. The turning point was realizing the truth about ho-mosexuality. We finally understood that our daughter never chose to have same-sex attraction. We came to realize that SSA resulted from many of her life experiences and perceptions about events.

The truth lifted the veil of ignorance from our minds and allowed our hearts to love our daughter the way that she needed. The truth has set us free. Sarah recently said, "I haven't felt your love in six years. I feel closer to you now than ever before."

When we understood that she wasn't born this way *and* did not choose to have SSA, we were able to move from anger and judg-ment to compassion and love. This was the greatest lesson we learned in the teleconferencing classes and by attending the LSI Healing Seminar. There we witnessed the wounded hearts of so many men and women who struggle with same-sex attraction. We gained such a greater appreciation for our daughter.

Most of us have been led to believe that people are born gay or lesbian. But this is not true. When we deeply understood this critical point, we began to love our daughter without reservation. Over the past months, we have spent so many days and nights listening to Sarah vent. Saying the magic words, "Thank you, Sarah. Tell us more," has allowed us to witness the tremendous pain of our daugh-ter. We have gone to hell and back with her and shall continue to do so as long as necessary. Our daughter is now bonding with us on a daily basis. She attends therapy regularly, and believe it or not, she is dating a fine young man! Yes, she is dating a *man*.

Sarah followed every step in recovery that we had learned. She was a textbook case. She said, "I was receiving emotional gratification from my girlfriend and not you, Mom. I never connected with you." She was in deep turmoil as she shared these things. We kept repeating, "Thank you, Sarah. Tell us more." What came out of her mouth was exactly what was taught. She said she felt rejected by me (Mom) and that I had left her all alone. If we had not understood the causes of SSA and how our daughter's unique temperament led to her perceptions, we would have been so defensive. But because we did understand that this is how *she* experienced the past, we could simply say, "Thank you, Sarah. Tell us more."

We would never have been able to do this in the past. We would have definitely spent the entire time defending ourselves and telling her why she was wrong. We learned how to use the magic words, "Thank you, Sarah. Tell us more," and they worked! We realized that we couldn't argue our daughter out of homosexuality. It is an emotionally based condition. It is all about wounds. And without healing, she could not change her behavior.

Today she is healing. She is opening up. She has come a million miles in such a short time. We had a chance to pull her out of this when she first came out to us. If we had known then what we know now, we could have helped her heal and prevented all these miserable things from happening. Because we did not understand the truth about SSA, and how our daughter thinks, we did all the wrong things. We all paid a dear price—she much worse than us. Now, no matter what she does or where she goes, we will love her unconditionally.

We are now involved with our local PFOX chapter and are sharing with them the wonderful things we have learned. We wish to help other parents so they don't make the same mistakes we did. We try to impress on them that they need to go to hell and back with their kids. There is just no other way. *This is a battle of love, and whoever loves the most and longest wins!*

Shortly after her parents wrote their story, Sarah faced the woman who abused her as a teen. At first, her parents thought she might become involved with her again. But Sarah saw how deeply wounded and bitter this young lady was. That was the greatest testimony to her about the un-happiness of the so-called gay life. After experiencing more healing in-dividually and with her parents, Sarah began dating. Eventually she met a wonderful man, and they married in the summer of 2006. Her parents were amazed at the transformation they all experienced.

STEP SEVEN
Discover Your Child's Love Language

If you haven't already, I suggest reading *The Five Love Languages* by Dr. Gary Chapman, which will provide you with important insights about your child's character. The term "love language" refers to the way we experience love as expressed by another person. Everyone has a primary and secondary love language. By investigating our children's love languages, we can better understand their character and ways to support their growth.

Here is a brief summation of the five love languages.[1]

Love Language 1: Words of Affirmation

1. *Offer verbal compliments.*

   a. Appreciate your child's *being,* or who she is (that is, her qualities and attributes). For example: "You are such a wonderful woman." "I appreciate your generous heart." "You are a very sensitive and gifted woman." "You're such a beautiful and feminine woman."

   b. Appreciate your child's *behavior,* or what he does (that is, behaviors that you like). For example: "You have such great taste in clothes." "I really appreciate your taking out the trash." "I admire your diligence in getting your homework done."

---

[1]From Gary Chapman, *The Five Love Languages* (Chicago: Northfield Publishing, 1995).

2. *Speak words of encouragement.* Try to see the world through your child's eyes. Learn what is important to him. "I'm excited that you're in the school play. I know you'll do a wonderful job."

3. *Speak words of affection.* "I love you." "You mean so much to me." Tone is important, especially to a sensitive child.

4. *Praise your child in front of others.* Speak affirming words about her in front of family members and other people. Tell her how wonderful she is.

5. *Write affirmations.* Write affirming notes, letters or e-mails to your child.

John was a good father, but spent little time with his eighteen-year-old son. When Robby "came out" to his wife and himself, John knew that *he* had to change. Realizing that Robby was a sensitive and talented young man, he immediately began to offer words of praise and appreciation: "Son, I think you're a great guy. I'm sorry I haven't been there as much as I should have been. Now I'm going to take more time to share and listen." Robby was angry, "Why now? It's too late!" Dad didn't give up. "I'm here now, and I'm not going to back away." He was persistent in his parenting. It wasn't easy.

John continued to praise Robby's character. "I think you are such a dynamite musician. I really enjoy hearing you sing. You have such a gift from God." The more he praised his son, in time, Robby softened. John found that speaking words of affirmation were a direct pathway into Robby's heart.

Love Language 2: Quality Time

1. *Togetherness.* Focus your undivided attention on your child and what she likes (not what you like).

2. *Quality conversation.* Use sympathetic dialogue and good listening skills, focused on what your child is saying—thoughts, feelings and desires. Do not analyze or problem-solve; just use reflective listening and often say, "Thank you, [child's name]. Tell me more."

3. *Use "I" statements, not "you" statements.* Learn to share your thoughts, feelings and desires without judging the other person. Teach and instruct rather than preach and lecture, which are immediate turn-offs. Note: If you are opposite personality types—Dead Sea (does not like to share) and Babbling Brook (cannot stop talking)—it is important to establish regular sharing times to create balance in the relationship.

4. *Share quality activities.* Provide wonderful memories that last a lifetime (for example, camping, hiking, attending a play or concert, going on a trip together). Participate in your child's interests.

Mike's primary love language is quality time. His dad wasn't acclimated to sharing or looking at him directly in the eyes. After some intensive family therapy sessions, Mike's dad stretched his heart and mind to join in his son's world. He learned to utilize good listening skills while establishing eye contact. They went on a camping trip together. It was heaven for Mike. His father also enjoyed the rich time together. "Dad, this meant the world to me," Mike said, "just you and I being together, sharing and laughing. I will always remember this trip."

Love Language 3: Receiving Gifts

1. *Gifts are meant to be an expression of love from the heart.* They are visual symbols of love for the other person.

2. *Find out what your child likes.* Investigate his desires and interests.

3. *Gifts may be purchased or made*. Spending on a child whose love language is receiving gifts will fill that child's love tank.

4. *Rituals or ceremonies*. Place value on the giving of your gifts, whether for birthdays, special events or just surprises. Gifts are an expression of your love, not just material objects.

5. *Give the gift of yourself*. Your physical presence is a powerful gift, especially in times of crisis.

6. *Receiving gifts is unearned grace*.

7. *Don't let yourself give gifts because of your feelings of guilt*. That is counterfeit giving.

Jane was heartbroken that her daughter, Jen, was in a long-term, committed relationship with another woman. This was diametrically opposed to her spiritual beliefs. Nonetheless she loved Jen, so she did what she had to do to sustain the relationship. Biting her tongue on many occasions, she listened as her daughter shared. Often there were tumultuous times between Jen and Lynn, her partner. Jen called her mom and said, "Please come. I really need you now."

Jane got in the car her and drove four and a half hours to her daughter's home. Then she comforted her and listened as Jen shared about her pain and anguish over the relationship. This went on for over a year and a half. Each time, Jane drove back and forth. The greatest gift Jane gave to her daughter was to "be there" for her when she hurt the most.

Eventually Jen woke up. She realized this wasn't how life should be. She separated from her partner and asked her mom for help. Jane proved that whoever loves the most and longest wins.

Love Language 4: Acts of Service

1. *Do something special that will benefit your child* (for example,

build something together, teach a skill, do homework together, work on a car). This is an investment of time, effort and thought. It's important for us to do things for our children that they cannot do for themselves, or to teach them something they don't know how to do but would like to learn.

2. *Help your child learn to make requests, not demands.*

3. *Ask your child to make a list of things he would like you to do for him.*

4. *A child's criticism is a clue to his love language* (for example, "I really wish you would teach me to throw a ball"). It is never too late to spend time with our children, whether they are five or fifty.

5. *Be available but don't be a doormat and let your children walk all over you.* They will not respect you if you do. Kids need bonding and boundaries, love and limits, and then they will feel safe and secure.

6. *Overcome stereotypes.* Bear in mind that SSA children are often very sensitive—something we fathers particularly need to remember. Dr. Dean Byrd gives excellent counsel to dads with young boys who like to play with dolls: "Get down on the floor and play with him and his dolls. After joining in his world, he will be more willing to participate in yours." It works.

Charlie was a teacher. He was great with kids, but he and his son, Tim, just didn't connect. Charlie had three other boys, and they got along great. Tim, like many SSA kids, was highly sensitive. Charlie looked long and hard for opportunities to connect with his son. Finally he found a common base: a car. Tim needed a car for work and school, so Charlie bought him an old Chevy that needed work. Together they rebuilt the engine and fixed the transmission. Spending time together working on Tim's car made him feel loved and special in his dad's eyes.

It's funny, Tim comes over to his folk's house often and asks Charlie, "Would you help me work on the car today?" It has become a place where father and son can meet and share.

Love Language 5: Physical Touch

1. *Physical touch communicates emotional love.*

2. *Babies need to be held, kissed, rocked, cradled and caressed in order to survive.*

3. *Adolescents and adults need lots of healthy touch in order to thrive.*

4. *Offer healthy nonsexual touch.* This may consist of holding your child's hand, hugging, putting your arm around her shoulder and more.

5. *Touch equates with emotional intimacy and love.* Be flexible. Follow your child's cue. Adult children may want to receive hugs or may want and need to be held.

6. *Healthy touch will help create secure attachment.* This is especially true for those dealing with SSA. Sons need their dads, and daughters need their moms.

7. *Many women and men who experience SSA are touch-deprived.* They hunger for healthy touch and end up going into the SSAD "gay" world to get their needs met.

Ellen was not particularly demonstrative. She had grown up in a house of all boys. Being soft and gentle was not easy for her around all that testosterone. Her mother never held her warmly in her arms. Therefore, when she gave birth to her own daughter Susan, it wasn't easy for her to display affection openly. This became a source of pain and longing in Susan's heart, mind, body and soul. As she grew and matured, same-sex desires increased. Ellen judged her for having homosexual feelings, saying, "You will go to hell if you practice this horrible behavior."

Luckily a pastor in their church had knowledge about helping kids with SSA. He met with Susan's parents and told Ellen that what Susan really needed was closeness—displays of warmth and affection. In time, and with much practice, Susan began to taste how it felt to be held by her mother. She began to grieve. "Mom, all I ever wanted and needed was you. I have been seeking your love in the arms of other women." Through continued times of holding and open displays of physical affection, Susan's heart began to melt as the pain poured out. After one year of continued efforts, Susan's SSA waned and today she is engaged to a young man.

Love Is Spelled with Three *T*s: Time, Touch and Talk

Time. Children love being with dad and mom, doing things together, sharing in activities. The most essential focus in this particular plan is father-son or mother-daughter quality time together. Participate in your child's interests.

Touch. All children, but especially sensitive ones, crave being held, embraced, hugged, stroked, caressed. Dad, your son needs to feel your warm embrace. I know this may be foreign, even frightening, for some fathers. You will need to practice appropriate physical affection with your son (see step eight for more details). If you struggle with this, it may help if you think of it this way: when it comes to touch, your son is going to get it somewhere—either from you or his boyfriend. Mom, you will need to do likewise for your daughter.

Talk. Your SSA child will respond warmly to conversations with dad and mom, being listened to, letting him know who you are and finding out who he is. Communication is like oxygen for a relationship. Without breathing, we die. Without communication, the relationship dies. Dad, make time for conversation with your son. Mom, reach out and listen to your daughter. You do not need answers; you simply need to be there to listen and share. Make it real.

By experiencing the three *T*s of successful parenting, a child will gain a sense of value, belonging and competency. Being valued is an inner belief that I matter, that I am special, valuable and unique. Belonging is an awareness of being wanted, accepted, cared for, enjoyed and loved. Competency is a feeling that I can do any task, cope with any situation and meet life without fear.[2]

Keep trying, even if you make a hundred mistakes. It shows that you care. And prepare yourself for rejection; it may happen, but never give up. Your child desperately needs you.

Investigate Your Child's Likes and Dislikes

Perhaps you already know about your child's interests. If so, do your best to get involved by participating in activities that she enjoys, even if it is against your nature. Even if you don't know her specific interests, you can always ask what she'd like to do—go to sporting events, see a movie, shop, do a jigsaw puzzle. Again, this is a mother-daughter or father-son project.

As you do things together, remember to be generous and consistent about offering words of praise and affirmation. Those who struggle with same-sex attraction often have a tendency toward low self-worth. So the more you praise and affirm your child's worth, the better he will feel about himself: "You're such a handsome boy." "You're an amazing athlete." "You are really strong!" Or affirm your daughter: "You're such a beautiful young woman." "I really admire you." "You have so many wonderful gifts."

Many of the dads I have counseled found a way to work on cars with their son, which provided a wonderful time of bonding for the two.

---

[2]From David Seamands, *Healing for Damaged Emotions* (Wheaton, Ill.: Victor, 1981), p. 60.

Other dads attended their sons' theatrical productions and cheered them on. Still others took their sons on camping trips. We need to create opportunities to spend quality time with our children, affirming their gifts and interests, drawing them closer to our hearts.

Focus on Activities That Emphasize Your Child's True Gender

Offer your child genuine praise every chance you can. The more sensitive he is, the more your comments will make a significant impact on his life. But be patient! It took time for him to develop SSA, so it will not dissipate in a week, month or year. Just be available and affirm your child each step of the way.

In males, SSA denotes a lack of masculine identity. No matter what their physical appearance may be, deep inside is an insecure little boy. This is where same-sex parents can make a huge difference. Dad, if possible go to the gym with your son and work out together. Mom, take your daughter clothes shopping. Spend a day at the salon or spa and affirm her beauty and femininity. SSA children need to internalize their same-sex parent's love and acceptance.

Read Your Child's Literature First

When your child gives you something to read, the best thing you can say is, "Thank you! Yes, of course I will read it." This helps communicate that you are seeking to understand your child's point of view. Whether you agree or disagree with the literature, it's important for you to remember that the goal is to create a secure attachment, not to pass judgment about what is right or wrong.

When you've finished, feel free to discuss what you've read. You need not lie or speak hypocritically. If you completely disagree, say so. But own your thoughts, feelings and opinions, and be sure not to make them into universal truths. Although some people with SSA are unable to handle mature discussions, you and your child may simply have to agree to disagree. He may react to your comments as if they were personal insults, fly off the handle and perhaps throw a temper tantrum. No matter—be forgiving. It helps to remember that this behavior is like that of a two- or three-year-old who lacks discipline and has not yet learned to regulate his emotions.

If there is an emotional conflict, let your child know that you love him, and try again another time. Above all else, be sure you reinforce this truth: *I love you just the way you are.* This is critical for successful bonding and establishing the love connection between you.

Share Your Literature with Your Child

Please don't read their pro-homosexual literature just so you can say, "Okay, now read mine!" By reading your child's literature, you demonstrate that you genuinely care and are interested in his point of view. Keep it real. Most likely he has seen and heard only pro-homosexual literature and ideas. If he has heard anything about healing from unwanted SSA, it was probably biased against such a possibility. Be patient with your child.

On the other hand, if you sense that your child is open to a different point of view, you may ask if she would be willing to read some publication, to watch a DVD with you or to review a book or an article of your choice. Of course we should not force our children to read or watch anything against their will. To do so would simply create more negativity and detachment. Remember, oppositional behavior is at play here. You are dealing with a wounded child. Ask yourself before doing anything, "Will this bring us closer or draw us further apart?" The goal of all we say and do is to create greater intimacy and more secure attachment. Chances are, no SSA child will be changed by reading a book, unless they are motivated to pursue healing.

Be very selective about what you give your child to read or watch, and don't offer too much at one time. Focus on one book or article, then ask for feedback. Wait a while, then offer another piece of literature. You might salt-and-pepper your approach: read something of his. Discuss it. Then offer something of yours. Discuss it. Keep the dialogue and exchange going. When you feel sure that you have established a strong alliance, you may find the freedom to say, "What I've learned is that you don't have to be gay. There is a choice." But please use caution, and if you aren't sure about what to say, err on the side of reticence. Remember, we must first win our children's hearts before changing their minds.

Once you've learned about your child's SSA, you will start to see the homosexual issue everywhere you look. It was always there, but now that it's personal, you suddenly find yourself paying more attention. Bear in mind that this is not a new subject to your son or daughter, who has been living with it for many years. You are the newcomer to the so-called gay world, not your child.

Attend Meetings of Their Choice

If your loved one asks you to attend a PFLAG, GSA or GLBT meeting, I hope you'll find the courage to go. Once again, do not attend in order to agree; you go to gain understanding. We would all be wise to walk a mile in our children's shoes, going where they want us to go and reading whatever literature they'd like us to read. It is essential that we learn about life from their point of view before we ask them to entertain the possibility of change.

Meanwhile invite your child to activities that may encourage and strengthen her. As Arthur Goldberg, the codirector of Jews Offering New Alternatives to Homosexuality, states, "JONAH encourages parents to bring their sons or daughters to their family and friends' educational meetings. This has been a successful strategy for some parents, particularly when their child can relate to one of the strugglers who may be presenting a testimony at the meeting."

STEP EIGHT
Same-Sex Parent, Display Appropriate Physical Affection

Many men who experience SSA are literally starving for affection. So it is very important for fathers to initiate some form of physical touch and to say, "I love you." I know this may be foreign to many men because they did not experience it with their own fathers. If that is the case in your family, it is time to make a change, and your son will help you. Men with SSA are often touch-oriented but touch-deprived. Touch is their primary love language, and because they haven't experienced it in healthy ways, they seek it in unhealthy ways. At the core, they crave male bonding.

If you have not done this before, let your son know that you want to express yourself more physically and that you intend to reach out to him. Be honest and let him know if it is difficult for you. Then begin doing it: hug him, hold him, kiss him. And when you hug your son, instead of saying, "Give me a hug," try saying, "I would like to give you a hug." You're the dad, and he is your son. You give, and he receives. Eventually it will become reciprocal.

Practice makes perfect, so don't give up. Your son not only wants, he also needs love and affection and he needs it from *you*. I do not exaggerate when I say that it could be a matter of his life or death. Remember that he may be looking for your love in the arms of other men.

This is an issue that I understand very deeply. I craved my father's affection. If only he had held me in his arms and said, "Richard, I love you, my son. I apologize for not hugging you and kissing you throughout the course of your life, and for not telling you how much you mean to me." I would have melted in his arms.

One way to make this change in your relationship with your son is to create new rituals. Hug him each time you greet him and hug him again before he leaves your home. Kiss him on the cheek and say, "I love you, [use his first name or whatever nickname he prefers]." Hold him in your arms. There are photos on page 207-8 of *Coming Out Straight* that shows a man holding a son and a woman holding a daughter. Even though it may seem out of the question or ridiculous to hold your grown-up son, it may be just what he needs.

Although my son doesn't suffer with SSA, he and I are healing our relationship. At one Father-Son Healing Seminar we sponsor yearly, he told me that all he wanted as a boy was for me to hold him in my arms. I asked him, "Would you like me to do that now?" He said, "Yes." During the seminar, as I embraced him, I was very aware of the peaceful feeling that came over him. We continue to be affectionate with one another.

Another father who attended the seminar with his two teenage sons said, "When I saw the photo in the book, I thought to myself, 'I would never do that with my sons.' But after holding each of them, it felt so natural. It brought me back to the time when they were kids." Both sons enjoyed their father's arms around them. One son is dealing with SSA and the other is not, but they both loved it. All human beings thrive on their parents' healthy expressions of love and affection.

You *can* make up for lost time. It is never too late to heal. If hugging another man is beyond your capacity, I suggest asking a friend, pastor, rabbi or mentor to help you learn. There are men who are comfortable with intimacy, and you may need to experience receiving their healthy touch before you can give it to your son.

All that I just shared also applies to many mothers and daughters. Women who experience SSA often crave healthy touch and emotional intimacy. The more mom provides such basic needs, the more her daughter will feel loved, and a stronger connection will be established.

Cautionary Measures

There may be instances when the parent-child use of holding, hugging or displaying physical affection is ill-advised. Such cases may be (1) if the child experienced physical or sexual abuse, (2) if the child experienced an invasive or emotionally incestuous relationship with his or her opposite-sex parent, or (3) if the child is not particularly touch-oriented. Never force the issue of healthy touch on a child who is unwilling to receive it.

If the child experienced physical or sexual abuse, it may be wise to first seek professional help before initiating any type of physical affection. It is imperative to be sensitive to his or her needs, because the child's boundaries were violated in the past.

If the child experienced an invasive or emotionally incestuous relationship (mother-son or father-daughter), the child may consciously or unconsciously blame the same gender parent for not protecting him or her from the emotionally close binding opposite-sex parent. Oftentimes, when a wife's emotional and/or physical needs for intimacy with her husband go unmet for a significant period of time, she may turn to her sensitive son to experience some kind of closeness. Of course, her motivation may not be to hurt the child. However, this has a profound and damaging effect on his psychosexual development. In essence, the mother uses her son to fulfill her unmet love needs, and thus he becomes a substitute spouse. This type of emotional intimacy and unhealthy touch creates a great fear of the feminine in the heart and soul of the child. Dr. Patricia Love calls this an "emotional incest syndrome."[1] The

---

[1]See her book of the same title: Patricia Love, with Jo Robinson, *Emotional Incest Syndrome: What to Do When a Parent's Love Rules Your Life* (New York: Bantam Books, 1990).

same type of enmeshment or incestuous relationship may have occurred between the father and his daughter.

If the child did experience this type of inappropriate closeness with the opposite-sex parent, he or she may hold a deep resentment toward the same-gender parent: "Why didn't you stop her?" "Where were you when I needed you?" "You didn't you protect me from her?" Therefore, if a father attempts to initiate holding or healthy touch with his son, the child may reject such behavior because of his underlying anger and hurt from the past. The same would hold true of a daughter toward her mother, because she too felt unprotected.

Regarding the third category, if your child is not particularly touch-oriented, this will take discernment. Those who experience same-sex attractions are out of touch with their inherent sense of gender identity. As we have discussed, this evolved over a period of time due to many influential factors, such as insufficient bonding with the same-gender parent, overattachment with the opposite-sex parent, lack of same-gender peer bonding, hypersensitivity, sexual abuse, body-image wounds and so on. As a result of these and other variables, much of the time she or he developed a defensive detachment toward the same-gender parent and peers. Therefore, your overtures toward establishing a healthy, salient relationship may necessarily meet with resistance. I will address this resistance in the following section. The main point here is to use your best judgment as to whether they are exhibiting a defensive detachment toward you because of past wounding or opposition because they are not touch-oriented in the first place. You may discuss with your spouse and other children to determine which issue is at play in this situation.

If your child or loved one was sexually or physically abused by any person, for example, a parent, relative, neighbor, friend; if there was an emotionally incestuous parent-child relationship; or if the child is not touch-oriented, please be cautious when suggesting or initiating healthy hugs or holding. This may be interpreted as manipulative and as a way to avoid dealing with unresolved issues in the family system. Again, in all instances assist your child's healing by seeking professional help for all family members involved.

Your motivation for offering the gift of healthy touch is paramount. Ask yourself the following question: *Am I doing this for my benefit, or that of my child?* Unequivocally it must be solely for the sake of your son or daughter.

Expect Rejection

Regarding the use of healthy touch with children who have not been violated or abused in the past, your attempts to express affection toward them may be met with rejection as well. Even though it is what people with SSA need, they may rebuff your attempts at intimacy. Why? Because deep inside is a hurt and angry little child demanding, "Where were you when I needed you? Why now? Why not then? I'm hurt and I won't let you in."

Mom, please don't accept your daughter's rejection. She needs you, and even though she rejects you time after time, she is waiting for you to break through her defenses and set her free. I appeal to you not to quit. Be patient and just imagine her as a hurt little girl each time you give her a hug. Imagine that you are speaking to the hurt little girl, not to your adolescent or adult daughter. Try to speak gently to that wounded child and say, "I love you, and I won't let you go." Dad, the same thing applies to you and your son.

One dad was regularly showing affection to his seventeen-year-old son. The son barely tolerated these times with his dad, and he always protested. After a year, when the father learned that his son was in a relationship with another man, he stopped trying altogether. But the son said to me, "I'm so angry with my father. Why did he give up on me?" Eventually he told his dad how disappointed he was, and—hard as it was—the dad began to reach out again (read their story at the conclusion of this step). Parents, I encourage you not to withhold your affection from your son or daughter—no matter what.

It's a Gender Identity Disorder

Let's review some important points: Same-sex attractions occur when people have an incomplete sense of their gender identity and therefore seek it in the arms of another person of the same gender. They are drawn to same-sex partners to complete their homo-emotional and homo-social stages of development.

All children need to bond with their same-sex parent, same-sex peers and same-sex siblings and relatives. Every expression of bonding is an emotional contribution to help build up their gender identity. It is never too late to change, to heal, to grow, to come into the fullness of one's true gender identity. It is all about resolving childhood wounds and fulfilling unmet needs for love in healthy relationships. When that occurs, opposite-sex desires often naturally ensue. But here's a key principle: *A man must bond with men before he can be a man with a woman, and a woman must bond with women before she can be a woman with a man.*

Normal needs for bonding and attachment in pre-adolescence are experienced as sexual yearnings after puberty. That is when the world tells them, "You are gay." And that is false. Men and women with SSA are simply looking for love, healthy bonding and intimacy with members of the same gender because they did not experience that in the early stages of child development and adolescence. And sex will never solve their needs for love and affection because SSA has very little to do with sex. Every same-sex attraction represents a broken heart.

You are the answer. Healthy father-son bonding, healthy mother-daughter bonding—these are some of the primary solutions to healing SSA. You do not need to worry about changing your child's mind about ideology. If you win the heart, you will win the mind too.

However, I need to insert a note of caution here: if there are unhealthy connections or over-attachment in the mother-daughter or father-son relationship in your family, they do need to be corrected. Is there some form of inappropriate intimacy, whereby the child is taking care of the parent's needs? If so, it will stand in the way of healing.

I counseled a young man named Joe who loved his dad with all his heart. He was literally his father's best friend, and in fact he was the only friend his father had. Joe's father was isolated and removed from healthy social interaction with other men, and Joe felt responsible for his father's well-being. Why? Because Joe lacked the strength to extricate himself from his unhealthy alliance with his father.

It's important for couples with SSA children to remember that the opposite-sex parent needs to take a backseat and defer to the same-sex parent (more about this in step nine). I know that may be difficult, but it will be well worth the effort necessary for change. Mom, you may act as a bridge between your son and his dad. Help your son go to his dad for affection and attention. Dad, help your daughter go to her mom for affection and attention. Both parents need to work together to set love in order, to set things straight.

Healthy Parent-Child Bonding

To help you identify your loved one's developmental needs, you find below a model first for male bonding, then for female bonding. This will show specific activities that are necessary at each particular stage of development. You may use this as a guide to retrace and realign the relationship with your child.

Stages of Male Development

First Stage: Bonding (0 to 1 1/2 years)

1. Parents hold the baby.

2. They gaze into his eyes.

3. They hold his head on their chest, letting him feel their heartbeat.

4. They touch his skin warmly.

5. They kiss him.

Second Stage: Separation/Individuation/Differentiation (1 1/2 to 3 years)

1. Parents hold the infant. The son feels safe in their arms, which establishes bonding and secure attachment.

2. They gaze into his eyes.

3. They touch and kiss him in a healthy way.

4. Father and son bathe together.

5. Father plays with his son, tossing him in the air, engaging in rough and tumble activities, horsing around.

6. Setting boundaries: Parents allow him to investigate (crawling and walking away) while setting appropriate boundaries for protection.

7. Child accepts parental controls yet also feels powerful enough to separate and individuate (he does not have to "take care" of his parents' needs).

8. Father allows son to be angry (for example, hears his anger about mom and helps neutralize friction in the mother-son relationship).

Third Stage: Socialization (3 to 6 years)

1. Father and son play games, sports, rough-and-tumble, wrestle.

2. Both parents hold and kiss him, reinforcing his secure attachment.

3. Father models healthy expression of feelings, teaches son how to regulate emotions, to express them in healthy ways and not project them on to others.

4. Father and son shower together, so son feels comfortable as a boy with his dad, "naked and unashamed," comfortable with his body. They also pee together, so the boy will not be pee-shy later on in the presence of other boys.

5. At this age a boy is often in love with mom (oedipal stage). Dad

needs to love Mom and help his son navigate through antagonistic feelings by modeling healthy husband-wife love and intimacy.

6. A boy needs to play with other boys to feel confident of his gender identity.

Fourth Stage: Pre-Adolescence (6 to 12 or 13 years)

1. Healthy touch between parents and son: Holding, arm around shoulder, hugging, holding hands, kissing.

2. Father and son shower together until son feels uncomfortable because of bodily and emotional changes (onset of puberty).

3. Father and son continue to play games, sports, roughhousing and wrestling.

4. Homo-social bonding: boy bonds with same-sex peers through sports, games, fun, roughhousing.

5. Son feels comfortable in the presence of his father and same-sex peers.

6. Father is the spiritual leader of the family, mentoring his son.

Fifth Stage: Adolescence (12 or 13 to 21 years)

1. Son internalizes father's masculinity.

2. He also internalizes same-sex peer friendships.

3. He feels masculine: "I belong."

4. He develops interest in the opposite sex.

5. Mom affirms son's masculinity and becomes his female mentor.

6. Sisters, aunts, grandmothers encourage son's masculinity by showing appropriate female love and affection.

7. Dad and mom model healthy male-female relations.

8. He courts women, respecting the feminine and learns more about the opposite sex.

9. His masculinity is affirmed through other male role models, such as coaches, teachers, pastors, rabbis.

10. He discovers and clarifies his sexual identity: a man among men, a man with a woman.

11. He graduates from the family, establishing his own identity, opinions and worldview.

Sixth Stage: Adulthood (21 to old age)

1. Seeks a mate.

2. Interdependence: Stands on his own, but reaches out when in need. Trusts self and trusts others.

3. Establishes his own family.

4. Loves his wife.

5. Loves his children.

6. Fulfills his purpose and mission in life through actively pursing goals and dreams.

7. Has good friends:

   a. Couples: shared activities as families.

   b. Relatives: shared activities as families.

   c. Male friends: mutual bonding and activities.

8. Gives back to others (community, nation, world). Mentors other men.

9. Maturity: relates as an adult (not as the child) with parents and in-laws.

Stages of Female Development

First Stage: Bonding (0 to 1 1/2 years)

1. Mother and father hold the baby.

2. They gaze into her eyes.

3. They hold her head on their chests, letting her feel their heartbeat.

4. They touch her skin warmly.

5. They kiss her.

Second Stage: Separation/Individuation/Differentiation (1 1/2 to 3 years)

1. Mother and father hold the infant. The daughter feels safe in their arms, which establishes bonding and secure attachment.

2. They gaze into her eyes.

3. They touch and kiss her in healthy ways.

4. Mother and daughter bathe together.

5. Mother spends time with daughter, participating in appropriate female activities.

6. Setting boundaries: Parents allow her to investigate (crawling and walking away) while setting appropriate boundaries for protection.

7. Child accepts parental controls yet also feels powerful enough to separate and individuate (she does not have to "take care" of her parents' needs).

8. Mother models healthy femininity and the joy of being a wife and mother.

Third Stage: Socialization (3 to 6 years)

1. Mother continues to reinforce daughter's femininity, encouraging healthy and appropriate female play.

2. Both parents hold and kiss her, reinforcing her sense of secure attachment.

3. Mother models healthy expression of feelings, teaches daughter how to regulate emotions, to express them in healthy ways and not project them on to others.

4. Mother and daughter bathe together, so she feels comfortable with mom, "naked and unashamed."

5. At this age, the daughter is often in love with dad (electra complex). Mom needs to love dad and help the daughter navigate through these feelings by modeling healthy husband-wife love and intimacy.

6. A girl needs to play with other girls to feel confident of her gender identity.

Fourth Stage: Pre-Adolescence (6 to 12 or 13 years)

1. Healthy touch between parents and daughter: Holding, arm around shoulder, hugging, holding hands, kissing.

2. Mother and daughter bathe together until daughter feels uncomfortable (going through body changes).

3. Mother and daughter play together, participating in female activities.

4. Homo-social bonding: daughter bonds with other girls through play, games and so on.

5. Daughter feels comfortable in the presence of mom and other girls.

6. Father is the spiritual leader of the family, mentoring his daughter.

Fifth Stage: Adolescence (12 or 13 to 21 years)

1. Daughter internalizes her mother's femininity.

2. She internalizes same-sex peer friendships.

3. She feels feminine: "I belong."

4. She develops interest in the opposite sex.

5. Father is important to affirm daughter's femininity and becomes her male mentor.

6. Brothers, uncles, grandfathers encourage daughter's femininity by showing appropriate male love and affection.

7. Dad and mom model healthy male-female relations.

8. She courts men, respecting the masculine, and learns more about the opposite sex.

9. Her femininity is affirmed through other female role models, such as coaches, teachers, pastors, rabbis.

10. She discovers and clarifies her sexual identity: a woman among women, a woman with a man.

11. She graduates from the family, establishing her own identity, opinions and worldview.

Sixth Stage: Adulthood (21 to old age)

1. Seeks a mate.

2. Interdependence: Stands on her own, but reaches out when in need. Trusts self and trusts others.

3. Establishes her own family.

4. Loves her husband.

5. Loves her children.

6. Fulfills her purpose and mission in life through actively pursing goals and dreams.

7. Has good friends:

   a. Couples: shared activities as families.

   b. Relatives: shared activities as families.

   c. Female friends: mutual bonding and activities.

8. Gives back to others (community, nation, world). Mentors other women.

9. Maturity: relates as an adult (not a child) with parents and in-laws.

If your child is young, you can use the information above as a road-map for parenting responsibilities. If your child is an adult, you may use it to identify stages in which important tasks for growth were missed. If you are unable to meet that need today, please be at peace. Ask God to provide other men and women to bless them.

As your child grows, Dad, you may want to consider limiting your time away from home in order to devote more attention to your son and to strengthen your bond with him. Mom, you might consider doing the same for your daughter. Children are a wonderful legacy. Spending time with them is the best investment we will ever make.

One Couple's Journey

My wife and I are Lutheran pastors. We attended a presentation that Richard made two weeks after our son told us, with much anguish and many tears, that he was attracted to the same sex. Although we believed that people were born that way, we did not want it to be so for him, because of the potential persecution and agony that he would undoubtedly endure in living out his inborn sexuality. But we never admitted to either one of our children that we had not been able to reconcile our belief with the Scriptures.

We went to hear Richard talk about understanding and healing homosexuality. We sat near the back so we could leave "if things got too weird." His impassioned testimonial about his thirty-year struggle with unwanted same-sex attractions touched our hearts and minds on a level never before experienced. Though we initially squirmed when he said, "No one is born with SSA, and people can change," this made sense of a lot of what we had experienced as a family while raising our son and our daughter. As we left the hall, we were speechless.

We purchased *Coming Out Straight,* and that night we went home and haltingly shared this radical new learning with our son. He was furious at our interest in this approach and extremely angry that we would even consider a new direction, but thankfully, he was willing to listen.

My wife and I read the book and found our family's reality described on most of its pages. How blind we had been! We had all wholeheartedly bought into the "born that way and can't change" myth. We realized, in fact, that this myth had permeated our seminary education and theological underpinnings. These new ideas challenged that myth. We also discovered a loving truth that accurately makes sense of the Scriptures. We knew that God was indeed a God of love and possibility, and not a God of ignorance or avoidance. We had avoided facing the truth that we could not reconcile with the Scriptures, but we also knew that love was the answer and not prideful judgment or shame. We had been uncomfortable with particular groups, churches and denominations that had called homosexuality a sin and said that it could be "prayed away." We knew that wasn't quite right either.

Although our son was very angry that we had done a 180, he was willing to read the book, and we could tell that he was finding meaning in some of the things that he was reading. Of the ten different potential variables mentioned in the book that cause SSA, we realized that we could relate to eight of them. We decided to proceed to the Washington, D.C., area for a family healing session with Richard. We were so grateful that our son was willing to attend.

It was one of the most incredible experiences of our lives. Though we have always cared for each other with a fierce love, we realized through family therapy that the dynamics of our relationship as husband and wife and pastor and pastor had profoundly affected our children. In particular, it had contributed to our son's same-sex attraction. Furthermore some of our wounds and childhood needs were excavated, and we began to see how these influenced our son's detachment from me and overattachment to his mother.

I began to come to terms with the fact that I had a distant relationship with my father. Because of that, I tend to remain at a distance or emotionally unavailable. That was my preferred method of coping as a child and later as an adult. My wife realized that she had come from a long line of matriarchs and that, in some cases, men were subtly emasculated. She had also experienced abandonment and rejection issues as a child, which led her to be a needy adult. She realized that she had inadvertently expected our son to take care of some of those needs. Family therapy exposed some of our blind spots and changed our lives in ways we never before imagined.

Although it was difficult at first, my wife took a backseat with regard to our family. At times she would be silent at the table and that allowed my son and me to converse in a way that we had not done before. As for me, I began to concentrate on being emotionally present. I practiced active listening and tried not to react, but rather paraphrase and respond with questions. I realized that it was more important for me to be in relationship with him than to be right all the time.

My own heart and self-care have been of foremost importance to the healing process. I was parented in unhealthy ways while growing up. Now I am getting in touch with my own inner child, and he is teaching me important lessons. I am learning to more fully celebrate the process of becoming the man God created me to be. My wife is keenly aware of becoming the woman God created her to be as well. We realized that our son's bravado in sharing his same-sex attraction was the release our family needed to begin the process toward healing and wholeness.

We finally got real with each other, and this allowed our son to begin to express his childhood wounds and unmet needs. He began to share his hell with us. He told us what it was like to sustain peer rejection and criticism. We knew he had a sensitive spirit and that both of our children were confused about male and female gender roles within the family. My wife and I are now taking responsibility for our past failures and our family is healing.

As part of our family treatment plan, I held my son several times a week. Most often, he just sat there, not wanting to be in my presence or arms. But I determined to win him back! In all honesty, it was exhausting. And there were many setbacks along the way. After one year of doing this, he found a boyfriend. So I thought, *Okay, this isn't working.* And I quit holding my son.

After one week he came to me and said, "Dad, I feel so hurt that you gave up on me and stopped the holding." I was shocked. I was humbled. And I determined not to quit this time, no matter what. And so we resumed our weekly holding sessions. Even though he still had a boyfriend, I fought hard to win him back. In time, that relationship did fall apart.

Our son graduated high school and went on to train with a professional theatrical company. He was steeped in the "gay" world but extremely unhappy. And then a miracle occurred. He met a wonderful group of men and women from a church that surrounded him with incredible love and affirmation. They invited him to move into a house with other youth group members. And so he did. More and more, while receiving the same-gender peer affirmation and attention he had never experienced in his life, we saw the walls around his heart melting day-by-day. Our son was coming alive; in fact he was blossoming and his faith was rekindled for the first time in years.

Now he is determined to heal from his SSA. He himself requested another family healing session to resolve the remaining issues he has with us and within himself. Recently he came home and has been sharing his newfound faith and freedom with his close friends. He even stood before the church congregation and shared his testimony of transformation. This new reality is a blessing beyond measure.

We are still dealing with our feelings of anger over the myth and how it ruins so many lives and robs so many people of their true personhood. We are grateful that we can harness some of that anger and channel it toward helping other people realize that *change is possible*. My wife and I are coming to terms with our new learning and reflecting on the way that the myth affected our family, our theological education and our church family. We have hope. Our family is now experiencing newfound joy, healing and wholeness. Thank God.

STEP NINE

Opposite-Sex Parent, Take Two Steps Back

The parent-child connection is the core relationship that rules the world. If it is strong and solid, we have healthy men and women. If it is broken and fragmented, we have a wounded world. In the preceding pages, we have been introduced to the idea that, when attempting to restore a secure connection with an SSA loved one, the opposite-sex parent should pull back from intense involvement with the child. At the same time, the same-sex parent should become more engaged with the son or daughter. Let's look more closely at how these ideas can be applied in families.

Mom, it is time to allow your son to share more of himself with his father. That means you do your best to make this happen. Begin by explaining to your son that your husband intends to be more involved in his life and that you encourage him to do the same. You can create a new alliance of love between your son and his dad by building a bridge between them.

At first your son may feel distressed because he thinks somehow the strong connection that has developed between the two of you will be at risk. He may experience this as abandonment. Let him know (using good communication skills, such as looking into his eyes, holding his hands and using "I" statements) that you love him and only want the best for him. You might say something like this: "It's important for you to be close with your father. I know that's difficult for you. Please, let him into your heart."

Then you may want to add the magic words "Please, honey, do it for me." These four words, "Do it for me," are very powerful. Every child, regardless of age, wants to please his parents. It is an instinct we all have because we need our parents' love. Do everything you can to help your son get together with his dad, or else he may spend the rest of his life looking for his father's love in the arms of other men. (The same applies for the SSA daughter. Dad, it is time for you to take a backseat and direct your daughter to her mom.)

Meanwhile, as you work with your son, you'll also want to support your husband. Encourage him to get more involved in his son's world, but please don't push, nag or coerce. He will then feel like a bad little boy and see you as the controlling mother. Be wise, as women so naturally are, and make him think that such good ideas must be his own. "Men may be the head of the body, but women are the neck!" commented the mother in *My Big Fat Greek Wedding*. (Again, Dad, gently encourage your wife to get closer to your daughter.)

One of the mothers in our teleconferencing class saw her new position as that of copilot instead of being the pilot and taking charge of everything. This can be a helpful metaphor for parents as they try to steer the ship into a new direction.

You Cannot Get Water from a Dry Well

One couple I counseled several years ago was strong in their religious beliefs and loved their four children with all their hearts. I suggested ways in which the father might get closer to his SSA son. Although he was a loving father, he was not a particularly emotional man, so he was resistant to doing the work necessary to reel his son in. Today his son is in a relationship with a man fifteen years his senior. This pattern frequently appears, demonstrating that the son is looking for an older, strong mentor to love and take care of him, a man who fills the role of an emotionally available father figure.

In this case, the mother was so frustrated with her husband's lack of effort that one day she exploded, "If he gets AIDS and dies, I will hold you partially responsible!" You cannot get more direct than that. I've heard for myself from many wives who become very troubled because their husbands do not do all they could to create a secure attachment between themselves and their sons. My humble suggestion is this: *wives, stop trying to get water from a dry well.*

If a father has the emotional capacity to give of himself, he would have done so by now. I suggest two things. First, step back to create a vacuum in the relationship with your SSA child. Here's one example: stop talking so much when the three of you are together. Your silence will create the necessary space for someone else to lead the conversation. Maybe your son and his father will start talking to each other. If they do, please don't interrupt.

Second, if your husband is unable to reach out to your son, find other men who speak your son's love language(s), for example, uncles, grandfathers, cousins or men from the church or synagogue. In the meantime, let go of the controls and quit demanding that your husband give of himself. You may want to talk to your pastor, priest or rabbi about helping you find trustworthy male role models for your son.

It took much time and effort to find the men who mentored me. My father did not have it to give. So I had to actively seek and teach men what I needed. I received about fifteen or more rejections before I found the three men who loved me to life. Without them I might not be alive today. This is a battle for the life of your child. Find mentors for your child who will be loving and supportive (see step twelve).

Affirm Your Child's Gender Identity

As you are strengthening your child's bonds with his same-sex parent, don't forget the encouragement. Mom, applaud your son. Tell him how masculine and powerful he is. Dad, praise your daughter. Tell her how beautiful, lovely and feminine she is. Girls and women, boys and men can never hear enough sincere compliments.

It is also important for parents to speak with respect about one another. Mom, do not make disparaging comments about Dad (or men in general) in front of your son. To the contrary, affirm your husband. Dad, do not insult or mock mom or women in front of your daughter. Instead speak lovingly about your wife. Moms are very important in creating healthy men, much as dads are essential in creating healthy women.

We all need to experience gender affirmation from our opposite-sex parent. This is especially critical in the adolescent years of psychosexual and psychosocial development. If you missed it then, don't despair, because it is never too late for your child to hear words of parental affirmation. And if you have been relying on your child for emotional support, it's time you had a serious conversation with him. Your message is, "You are not responsible to take care of me." Set your child free to be who he is. We are here to take care of our children, but they may have misperceived who the caretaker really is.

A Mother's Story

When we were invited to our pastor's office, we knew our son Andy was having some sort of difficulty with this church, which he had attended for over twenty years. Andy had been in a Bible study with our pastor. They had memorized chapters of the Bible together and developed a strong friendship. But now my husband, Jim, and I saw a change in Andy's church attendance, and he no longer attended the Bible study. He seemed to have anger toward the pastor and the church in general.

What we heard that day left us numb with shock and full of confusion. We learned that Andy was involved in a relationship with a young man in the community. Our pastor had tried to help him and had encouraged him to talk to us about the abuse he had suffered at the age of fourteen when he spent time with Adam, his youth leader, at Adam's home. When the pastor asked Andy why he had not told us about the incident, he indicated that he was in some kind of bondage that kept him from discussing it with us. The pastor asked Andy, who is now a fire fighter, to confront the youth leader, but he did not have the courage to do that.

When Jim confronted Adam in the pastor's office, it was one of the hardest things he had ever done. Adam had become Jim's closest friend over the past fifteen years. The shock of these revelations lasted for more than a year. We made lots of mistakes, but we did some things right, including building a support team to talk to and pray with. Our pastor fasted and prayed with us for forty days. He came to our home often to share and to help us through the difficult days.

We learned everything we could about SSA and sex abuse. We attended a Love Won Out conference that helped us, but we needed assistance for our family and ourselves. After counseling with two different therapists, we were thankful to find some real help in the book *Coming Out Straight*. For the first time, we had questions answered, and we understood more about the incident and how it derailed him on his road to manhood in his early teens. We stopped blaming ourselves and each other, and started working on solving the problem.

One of the most helpful experiences was taking the Parent's Teleconferencing Class. We had our doubts, but eventually sought counseling from Richard. Jim was a self-proclaimed "homophobe." As much as he loves our son, he felt he could never accept him as he was. He felt uncomfortable spending time with Andy and his friends. He often felt so discouraged that he struggled with depression.

I was amazed at Jim's change of heart after the first session. We found help in many areas, mostly in communication with Andy. We learned it was important to listen to our son and ask questions. As part of our homework, we have written a plan for healing for our family. I have a prayer partner who prays with me daily for Andy. We have learned we need to share our experiences with friends and family members we trust. We are working on helping Jim and Andy build a strong father-son bond. They are hoping to go to a Father-Son Healing Seminar in Baltimore in August.

Andy has come to enjoy his dad's hugs. Jim is learning to express his love verbally. Andy is once again memorizing Scripture and asks me to pray with him. He is playing hymns on the piano. We continue to visualize him whole and free of SSA. We have a long way to go but no longer feel helpless and out of control. We are able to talk to people about same-sex attachment disorder and help them understand the truth about the problem. We are thankful to God for his leading, and today we are helping a support group in our church for men with SSA.

Section Three
COMMUNITY
HEALING

Section three is about building a base of supporters for the purpose of winning this battle of love. We must educate our family, friends, spiritual leaders and community about the truth of same-sex attraction: *No one is born with SSA; no one chooses to have SSA; and change is possible.* The lives of our loved ones are at stake, and the way we respond to men and women with SSA is critical. We need to demonstrate a higher love. We need to reach out and embrace them. "Greater love hath no man than that he lay down his life for his brother."

- Step Ten: Create a Welcoming Environment in Your Home, Place of Worship and Community
- Step Eleven: Boyfriends, Girlfriends, Ceremonies and Sleepovers
- Step Twelve: Find Mentors and Mentor Others

STEP TEN
Create a Welcoming Environment in Your Home, Place of Worship and Community

Because religious institutions and society have inflicted such heavy judgment on SSA men and women, they have found solace and compassion among themselves and those who affirm their homosexuality. We can reverse this unhealthy trend by creating safe, warm and welcoming homes, places of worship and social institutions. Otherwise the homosexual community will continue to be the only "safe" haven for our SSA children to experience love and understanding. As you work to build bridges with your SSA child, you will want to find ways to educate your family, friends and members of your faith about the causes of SSA and the possibility of change. Offer them books to read, websites to view and DVDs to watch.

As we've seen, over the past four decades, homosexual organizations have indoctrinated the general population into the myth that people are "born gay and cannot change"—part of a strategic plan to garner complete acceptance of homosexuality because of the painful persecution SSA men and women have experienced. It is up to us to reeducate our families and communities about the real facts of SSA. We need to turn this situation around by sharing the truth in love about why homosexuality exists and how change occurs—embracing those with SSA. Love is the ultimate weapon to win the hearts of SSA men and women who have felt, for so long, on the outside looking in.

I once counseled a man who was beaten by his father for most of his childhood. Whenever he was angry, the father would beat the son with his belt buckle. My client stated, "He wouldn't stop until he grew tired." With welts and bruises, he would crawl to his room and go under the bed to feel the cool cement alleviate some of the pain from his bloody body. His dad would often call him "faggot," "queer" and "sissy." Miraculously this man was able to escape his living hell, get married and have children. However, his SSA continues to haunt him. His same-sex attractions are a way of getting his attention in order to bring reconciliation and relief from those years of torment and pain. He has sought refuge in the arms of other men, but does not want sex. If only men in the church and synagogue would surround him, reach out to him and pour their affirmation, acceptance and affection into his hungry soul, how quickly he would heal.

As you reach out to your community on behalf of your loved one, explain why your son or daughter has SSA and ask them to surround your child with higher love. Give them specific instructions about how they can help your child heal through (1) healthy touch, including lots of hugs, (2) spending time participating in the things she cares most about, and (3) showing genuine concern for her well-being on a regular basis through calling, visiting or e-mailing.

Because you understand the basis of your child's SSA, you may now engage in activities centered on developmental needs and the healing of unresolved wounds. If your daughter was ostracized by other girls, allow loving women to surround her with positive affirmations. If your son did not fit in with the other guys, ask men to invite him out or participate in his interests. Have them help to reverse the curse and heal his wounds through the power of love expressed through the three Ts: time, touch and talk. This is a battle for the very heart and soul of your loved one.

Although you need to educate yourself sufficiently about the causes and healing of SSA, you don't need to be an expert in the field. Just speak from your heart with your support team about what you have learned and experienced and about how they can help you and your child. Your SSA loved one may have already found supportive and affirming organizations to help him or her accept their homosexuality. There are school, college, religious and other pro-homosexual organizations embracing your child and SSA. It is up to us to create alternative organizations where our loved ones can share their heartaches and be welcomed without affirming their SSA. Our children have experienced the misguided support. Let's work with others to create a wholesome, healing and godly support system.

Help Find Healthy Same-Sex Peers to Befriend Your Child

I have heard many stories from parents about their lonely SSAD sons and daughters: they don't fit in at school; they don't have many or any same-gender friends; they mostly hang out with opposite-sex friends. And then it happens. In high school, or even in middle school these days, they meet the "gay crowd" or attend the local GSA (Gay Straight Alliance) and—abracadabra—they have an instantaneous network of loving friends. Misery loves company, and now they have someone to commiserate with. These kids felt like lepers, and finally they are "home." They have someone to share with who understands their heartaches and pains, the longings and loneliness—another gender-confused person who has been through what they have been through. Their world will never be the same.

This is the indoctrination and enrollment of our children into the mythology of homosexuality. What can we do about it? I have coached numerous parents who actively pursued healthy peers for their children and won the battle. I know it is not easy. I know it will take lots of time, energy and wise planning. But it is possible. It can be done.

One place to start is to enlist your religious community. Ask a youth pastor for help. Get together with other parents and request their assistance and that of their children. Work behind the scenes with relatives and ask same-sex cousins, uncles, aunts and grandparents to find new ways to befriend your child.

You may also find same-sex peers who have come out of homosexuality. Ask for mentors from ministries and organizations assisting men and women in the process of change (go to <www.pathinfo.org>). Besides the same-sex parent, same-sex peers are the most important and influential to an individual's sense of gender identity. School buddies, cousins and friends from youth groups are key in the healing process.

Of course you may experience some rejection from family, friends and even your place of worship as you make these strategic efforts. Expect it. Some, perhaps many, will turn you down. Please don't give up! Your child is worth the effort.

Educate Your Religious Leaders About SSA

When you meet with your religious or spiritual leaders, you may find yourself in the role of teacher, helping them understand the dynamics of same-sex attractions. You will probably find that some of them have been indoctrinated into the "innate, immutable" myth. Most religions are divided straight down the middle on this issue. Either they reject those who experience SSA or they are completely accepting of them and their behavior. Unfortunately very few embrace these individuals because they understand the truth about SSA.

Give your rabbi, pastor or priest books to read and DVDs to watch. Religious leaders usually are busy people, so you will have to be sensitive, selective and persistent with your request. Perhaps you could invite them over to your house to watch a DVD. Make it as easy as possible for them to learn about this new perspective. It is to their advantage to receive such education, because—whether they realize it or not—many people in their congregation are dealing with SSA one way or another.

Once your pastor, rabbi or priest understands, you might consider asking him or her to address this issue from the pulpit.

When I spoke at a large church in Omaha, Nebraska, I cannot tell you how many people came up to me after my presentation and said, "My dad left us because of his SSA." "My son has SSA." "My former husband has SSA." "My brother has SSA." "My teacher at school is homosexual." "My parents are a same-sex couple." "My father is a transsexual and in the process of changing his gender," and on and on. And this was an average, Middle American church congregation. There are so many among us who have relatives and friends dealing with SSA, but very few are talking about it. This is happening everywhere, in every church and synagogue throughout the world.

Prejudice is an emotion. You will not quell bigotry through reason alone. You must show your heart and express your feelings of love for your SSA child. Personal stories are the best way to change someone's opinion. Rational arguments will not change anyone's mind, at least not at first, not when it comes to homosexuality. There is too much emotional baggage surrounding this issue. We need to begin by speaking on the personal level, then later present facts and information.

Join or Create a Support Group in Your Area

You will find strength and encouragement if you join a local support group, such as PFOX (Parents and Friends of Ex-Gays and Gays), JONAH (Jews Offering New Alternatives to Homosexuality), Exodus International (Christian), Evergreen International (Mormon), Encourage (Catholic), and other PATH members (see a more extensive list of international resources in the back of this book).

A Story of Victory

In his own words, Lee shares how he saved his son's life. He began implementing this plan when Tom was a junior in high school. It is a remarkable journey that gives hope to all. Today Tom is flourishing in his masculinity and heterosexuality. This proves without a doubt that people are not born with SSA and change is possible!

■ ■ ■

When Tom told me he was gay, I thought that it was not my fault, that genetics was really the problem. I thought I was a good dad. So I didn't say anything at first. I told my wife what he had said, and for the next few nights she'd cry herself to sleep.

For most fathers, there are probably several ways to look at the problem: (1) ignore it and believe it will just go away, (2) embrace it and join PFLAG (Parents and Friends of Lesbians and Gays), (3) kick the child out of the house, or (4) find a way to help your child understand what homosexuality is, how it occurs and how to work with the issue in a loving and caring manner without losing your child.

Now, several years later, I can say I have seen all of the above. I have spoken with parents in the quiet recesses of empty classrooms, at backyard barbecues and while sitting on benches watching sons and daughters sing and dance. All of them intrinsically know that homosexuality is not genetic, but they don't know what to do. I was just like them in the beginning.

I am good at one thing, and that is planning. But before I planned, my wife and I did some research. We went to the Internet, we went to the library, and we talked. We decided that we would love our son but would not endorse homosexuality or homosexual practices.

I bought every book I could on leaving homosexuality. I bookmarked every website, and I went to see a psychiatrist. Not Tom, me. I found a doctor who worked with sexual reorientation therapy. Dr. Frank was an older gentleman with whom I spent three sessions learning to understand my son. He told me what he had counseled other parents to do. He also advised me to deal with my own feelings, which I did.

After that, armed with books, pamphlets, printouts and most of all prayer, I built a plan to help my son.

I was a lousy Christian. I had read a ton of books, from C. S. Lewis to Os Guinness, but my faith was weak. So once again my wife and I began to attend church. We studied the Bible and showed our son that faith and belief are part of being a man and part of being a family.

So there I was. I read all the books on SSA that I could get my hands on. I talked things out with my wife. I prayed and thanked God for my wonderful son and family. I spoke with Tom's older brother and got his input. I implemented a systematic plan to get my son back. And it worked!

After two years of implementing my plan, I now have a son who no longer spends thirty minutes in front of the mirror or has to have clothes from a particular shop. He now clomps around and acts like a male adolescent seeking independence and not like a sulky, sullen kid. He also plays catch with his male friends and dates girls. Real dates, not shopping with the girls, as he used to. He even gets irritated with girls and says, "I don't get her. She acts so weird." He also helps around the house, mows the lawn, changes oil in the car, helps hang shelves and barbecues with me.

How did we do it? The plan we put into practice was based on a few things: My wife had to go into the background and defer to me. That was probably the hardest part of the plan, because she is strong and willful. She was the head of the household but was willing to abdicate her throne. Easier said than done. But she started saying things like, "Talk to your father first. If he says okay, then it is okay." She supported my decisions. When I used to say no, Tom would go talk to his mom and she would say yes. Well, that became, "If Dad said no, well then he's got his reasons. Did you ask him why he said no?" And so Tom would have to come talk to me, and my word would be upheld. No became no, and yes became yes. In time, when Tom wanted to do something, he would ask me, explain his reasons, and we'd talk. I most often said yes, because he was responsible. But I always knew where he was and who he was with.

I asked Tom to forgive me for not including him in the things I did, for leaving him out. He forgave me in a very tearful scene. Not easy.

I am a workaholic, and I also like to find quiet time away from everything. I really like to be outdoors. But I cut my work schedule back from sixty hours to forty-five hours a week and cut my activities. And I got Tom a job at the company I worked with so I could spend time with him on the way back and forth to work. For two years, in the summer, we went to work together . . . and we just had regular chats.

I spoon-fed information to Tom to counter the GSA (Gay-Straight Alliance at his school) influence and the "innate, immutable" lie. I started by saying, "You know, being gay isn't genetic. It's environmental." Then I would recommend a website to him. Later I would ask, "What do you think?" Usually I'd get, "Well, it was interesting." And then he'd add, "Well, do you think that change is possible?" I told him yes and referred him to websites that contained research that documented change.

I would have these types of conversations with him a couple times a month, but not every day. In other words, "being gay" was not the only point of conversation. I was trying to rebuild my relationship with my son. I also went along with my son to his voice lessons, and he would have to pick me up at the fly-fishing shop where I spent an hour or so. I have a great friend there whom I told about Tom's SSA, and he agreed to help me. So when Tom came in, this bear of a man would clasp Tom about the shoulder and ask how his singing went. He too used to sing a lot. At first Tom was a bit uncomfortable, but my friend never relented and, in fact, had Tom baby-sit for his son. He was the first adult male to give Tom a swat in the butt, I think for good grades.

I also enrolled Tom's brother, who started to call and talk to him— usually just guy stuff. He also started taking him to places like batting cages and roller-blading. This was all part of my plan to incorporate trusted friends and family to help my son.

In the beginning Tom used to hang out with kids from the GSA. When they called, I would not tell him. (So I'm a big meanie here, but Tom had a lot of schoolwork, outside obligations and a job as well. We encouraged him to continue to keep his platter full. He still does to this day.) I did not say he could not hang out with these kids. Peer groups can be funny things, and I knew that if I said, "These kids are bad for you," he'd probably continue to hang with them. So I would answer the phone and tell them he wasn't home. I encouraged Tom to see his old friends who were not gay and whose families I had known for a long time. I encouraged the dads of these friends to talk to Tom and so on. I never told them that Tom thought he was gay. I just said, "Hey, Bob, you're an accountant. You ought to talk to Tom. He's getting ready to look at a job, and maybe he'd like what you do." So I encouraged a lot of males to start sharing with him.

A physical relationship was also in order. I began to give him a hug and a kiss as I dropped him off at school. I used *Coming Out Straight* as a guide for what was appropriate and when it was appropriate. At first Tom was a little standoffish. Now he's hugging a lot of guys when he says good-bye, and these are straight guys. He has also gotten comfortable playing catch, and while I'd like it if he'd take up fishing, I can wait (I'm an avid fisherman).

Nowadays he seeks me out to give me a hug and a kiss good-night. It's like he needs to be reassured that this is okay between father and son. I also crack his back, and we roughhouse from time to time. He and his brother also wrestle when the older brother is home. All in good fun. But all important. So I yell at them and tell them to knock it off before they tear up the living room. Or to take it outside if they're going to do that stuff. My wife sits quietly by during these times and later will express her displeasure over these things but knows that they are important.

One day my wife said to me that Tom felt I was crowding him, so she asked me to back off. I told her that he'd have to tell me that. To this date he has not said that I'm encroaching on his territory. He does include me in his chats, his feelings, to a degree. My family is not big on discussing feelings, but we do talk about moral choices. About God's absolute rules. We do discuss issues, and we talk about making good choices.

These were not easy things to do: asking my wife to take a backseat, cutting my hours, committing time to my son, rebuilding a relationship and confiding in friends to help. I did make a mistake by asking a girl whom Tom had told that he was gay if she would talk to me about the issue, because I believed that she could help him become straight. She said that she would never help someone go from gay to straight, because it would harm them, that she supported all forms of human sexuality. To which I replied, rather callously, "Does that include pedophilia, bestiality and all other abnormal sexual behaviors?" I then apologized and said that I would not talk to her about it again. I also told Tom what had happened and apologized, asking for his forgiveness. It is something I caution all parents against. Be aware of who you talk to, and if possible, never mention this to other teenagers. It is not recommended unless there is some kid that you can trust implicitly.

I also used what I had learned from one of my mentors. I taught Tom how to use tools, how to make things with his hands, how to mow the lawn, how to change washers in a faucet, how to hang shelves. I made myself available to him. I kept all my promises and was there to support all his activities and to show him that a man can sing and dance and be a man. I supported him in learning to throw and hit a baseball. Just this year we watched a baseball game together. It was really a cool experience. We go to the hardware store and get nuts and bolts for little projects. I taught him how to make scones and other things as well. So I shared some of what I had learned from my mentors. I still can't get him to go fishing yet! I think this is because of his mom, who for years has harped on my fishing . . . well, he might still think that she disapproves.

So at the end of two and half years, what has happened? Tom is not gay. He has said so. All the gay literature is gone from the house. No gay friends call. He has actually decided not to be in plays and shows, saying he doesn't need to. He also said that he feels that he likes girls, but not like his friend Tim likes them. Tim has a very steady relationship with a girl, and they are probably sexually active. Tom has a girl that he likes quite a bit, but he doesn't want to get too involved. He knows what a morally correct, Christian relationship is, and we encourage him not to get too involved.

He is no longer effeminate. He wears ratty blue jeans, swears on occasion and lost the girly walk. He calls the GSA group a dangerous crowd, and he's doing well in school. His older brother says, "Don't worry, Dad. The plan is working. He's going to be all right." His brother has come to visit him at college, calls him regularly and sends him a gift from time to time. Tom is involved at church. At school he leads retreats and his new roommates are all jocks of some sort. From basketball to rowing, he's got three straight guys who whack him on the shoulder, and he whacks them back. When Tom is home, his old buddies hang out at the house, and he plays catch with them or goes out to do stuff with them.

My wife likes me to be in charge of things now. I like it too. Things became more complete when we put the plan into place. It is not easy. It takes love and dedication, and you feel like you're pouring all of yourself into this child. But in reality, you're giving this child what he needs: a dad, a male presence, a sense of order, a sense of masculinity. You're helping to make a new man, and it changes you as a person. Some of his "sweetness" rubs off on you, and your maleness flows into him.

I must admit that Tom is a different person from two and a half years ago. He lounges on the furniture, he gives off the attitude of being the dominant male in the household, he is not so sweet and nice, and in all honesty . . . well, at times I miss the "nice, sweet" kid. His mother wants to swat him from time to time, and he and I have our disagreements. He gets kind of lazy about his room and clothes, and things get flung around now. He threw a ball at me from the living room to the dining room, he dresses like a refugee from a thrift shop, and he never wears shoes if he can help it. Instead he prefers a pair of ratty flip-flops. He leaves wet towels lying around and sits around in his boxers watching Saturday morning cartoons or playing video games.

Yes, it's been an interesting time—a great time for mom and dad. And now I've got my son. God blessed this family as we kept God in the forefront of all we did with daily prayers and hopes and also asking others to pray for Tom. I know that there are miracles, and this is one of them. God answers prayers in a lot of ways, but I believe that he honors hard work, a changed heart and a loving family.

STEP ELEVEN
Boyfriends, Girlfriends, Ceremonies and Sleepovers

If your SSA child is still living at home, do your best to get to know her friends. If she is an adult and living away from home, getting acquainted with friends will, of course, be much more challenging. Any efforts you make along these lines are best done in a friendly, nonintrusive way: "I want to get to know you better, and your friends too." As she begins to talk about one friend or another, you might ask, "What is it about your friend that you like so much?"

Take the time to meet these friends. Invite them over. You may wonder, "Is this one SSA? Is that one straight?" I suggest that you let those types of thoughts go. Remember, those who experience SSA are hurt children who need love. It is all about compassion and genuine concern. The more we listen to our children and their friends, the better we will understand and appreciate them. Dad, please be sure you are acquainted with your son's friends, and Mom, do the same for your daughter.

Embrace Your Child's Boyfriend or Girlfriend

If your child has a same-sex girlfriend or boyfriend, my advice is that you go out of your way to meet, embrace and love this person. This is someone else's son or daughter. All SSA kids are wounded and looking for love. I know this may be one of the most difficult things for you to do—perhaps the yuck factor will rise up from the depths of your soul. Do your best to get over your recoil. Take a deep breath and try to see beyond the adolescent or adult to the child within. What you are really looking at are two little boys or two little girls seeking to fulfill their gender identity through one another. The problem is, neither one of them has solved this identity crisis! With your warm presence, you can be the bearer of great treasures for both of them. Be compassionate, be generous and be as loving as you can. *Love them both.*

It bears repeating that by getting to know your child's partner, you can figure out what needs your child is trying to fulfill through such a person. If she has an older partner, for example, then she has a need for being parented. If it is a same-age partner, he is trying to absorb or inherit characteristics that he feels detached from within himself. If the partner is younger, then she is trying to parent or love herself through another person, or attempting to heal unresolved issues from that period in her life.

Many women have been deeply hurt by men and therefore turn to women for their need for affection. Some are looking for mothering, others for someone to mother. Again, SSA is about gender detachment. They are looking to join with someone of the same sex to meet childhood emotional needs for bonding and intimacy, or they may be fleeing from intimacy with someone of the opposite sex because of hetero-emotional or hetero-social wounds. Some are drawn to the weaker or more wounded types. They are excellent caretakers. Basically they are giving to others what they hunger for themselves. They are just too frightened of trusting anyone or losing "control."

The more you reach out and embrace your child's partner, the closer you can grow to your SSA child. When you embrace your daughter's partner, with your daughter knowing full well that you completely disagree with the homosexual lifestyle, it shows the power of your unconditional love. Again, love them both.

On the other hand, when you embrace her partner, this may make her furious! Remember, at the core of this condition is an attachment disorder. So if you embrace your daughter's girlfriend, it may upset her because part of the SSA condition is oppositional behavior—"You hurt me, and now I'm going to hurt you!" Your loving her "partner" may upset her because she unconsciously wants to hurt you through her same-sex activities. When that doesn't work, she asks herself, "What's that about?" Be persistent and consistent in loving both your child and her "partner." It may just fracture the relationship. True love has the power to heal imperfect love.

Attend Your Child's Same-Sex Commitment Ceremony?

This is a difficult issue, and my ideas are not going to be accepted by everyone. Just keep in mind that what we are striving for in all these things is open communication and higher love. Here are two approaches that you might consider.

The first is to attend their commitment ceremony. A conversation may go something like this: "Son, you know that, based on our values, we do not approve of homosexuality. However, we love and accept you as you are today. We know that you are very happy with your partner, and therefore we are happy for you. That is why we choose to attend your commitment ceremony. Please know how much we love you both. We will always stand by you, no matter what. And please know that this is very difficult for us. It is not what we had envisioned for your life. But we love you, Son, and no matter how difficult it is for us, we will stand with and for you, now and forever."

The second approach is not to participate in the ceremony. I suggest that you lovingly share your truth with your child. Let her know that it is about you, not her—that the limitation is on your side, not hers. You may say something like this: "We cannot attend your commitment ceremony. As much as we love you both, it is simply too difficult for us to endorse this ceremony. We believe in you. However, we do not believe that two people of the same gender are meant to live as a married couple. We hope you will understand."

You will need to work through your thoughts and feelings individually, as a couple and perhaps with other supportive family members, friends and support group members. Pray deeply and ask God for guidance. Again, this is an issue of love, and love supersedes the law. Laws were created to serve humankind; humankind was not made to serve the law. Take time to make up your mind. Do not make a quick emotional decision. Your behavior greatly affects your child's life. Look at this issue from many angles.

I attended a conference where I heard a former lesbian share her testimony of transformation (let's call her Jennifer). Jennifer had been in a long-term relationship and had a commitment ceremony with her partner. One of her best friends attended, even though she was a strong Christian woman. This friend said that she loved Jennifer, and even though she disagreed with her lifestyle, she would stand by her through thick and thin. When Jennifer's relationship with her partner fell apart, her Christian friend was there to help her pick up the pieces. And it was through her love that Jennifer began to heal and come out of homosexuality. Remember, *whoever loves the most and longest wins!*

Sleepovers

The key here is being consistent with your standard of values. Would you allow your son to bring a girlfriend home and have her sleep in his bed? If not, then you would be inconsistent if you allowed his boyfriend to do the same. Maintain the same standard with either a boyfriend or girlfriend. When you do so, your child may be angry with you but will respect your integrity. Here's a suggested way of communicating: "Son, if you want your boyfriend to stay over, you and he need to sleep in different rooms. We would maintain the same standard if it were your girlfriend."

STEP TWELVE
Find Mentors and Mentor Others

One way you can help your SSA child is to find same-sex mentors for her. If you are a single parent, or if your spouse is unavailable or incapable of mentoring your SSA child, it is important to find men or women who will demonstrate healthy paternal or maternal love. You may want to ask relatives, friends and people from your place of worship to assist. I hope you'll find a way to surround your child with positive gender role models. Author and therapist William Jarma calls these very important people "Second Chance Fathers" or "Second Chance Mothers."[1]

Most of the men I have counseled had to create a network of mentors because their dads were unable to rise to the task as well. Since your child's needs may be great, enlist the support of several mentors. Each one may contribute his particular strength (such as sports, spirituality, warmth and healthy touch, fishing, car mechanics). The more mentors with varying abilities, the better.

Roles and Responsibilities of the Mentor

Those who did not experience successful attachment, love and intimacy with their father and/or mother seek to fulfill those unmet needs in other relationships or activities. Mentoring is a means whereby one may restore the parent-child relationship.

Three areas will need to be addressed in the process of mentoring:

---

[1]William J. Jarema, *Fathering the Next Generation: Men Mentoring Men* (New York: Crossroad, 1994).

1. Break down the walls of detachment. The mentor will need to be persistent and win the adult child's heart.

2. Develop healthy patterns in same-sex relationships, learning to be a woman among women or a man among men.

3. Experience healthy touch. Again, many with SSA are touch-deprived.

The adult child will work through three developmental stages while being mentored:

1. Dependence: a natural, healthy reliance on a parental figure.

2. Independence: learning to stand on her own feet.

3. Interdependence: knowing when to take care of herself and when she needs the help of others. Finally, she will grow into mutuality, giving back to the mentor and others.

Some of the roles and responsibilities of the mentor are

1. Knowing the child's love language and blessing her in those ways.

2. Providing healthy and healing touch.

3. Teaching skills and playing together.

4. Assisting in the grieving process.

5. Speaking words of affirmation and encouragement.

6. Disciplining her, establishing healthy boundaries and teaching emotional self-regulation.

7. Blessing the child for her special gifts.[2]

---

[2]Chapter twelve of *Coming Out Straight* details the process of mentoring.

It may be necessary to have several mentors, as one person will not have all that she needs. Again, each mentor imparts her special gifts to the SSA child.

Mentoring Other Men and Women with SSA

It will be a double blessing when you mentor someone else's child who experiences unwanted SSA. You can love your own child by loving another child. So many men and women with *unwanted* SSA are trying to find mentors, yet few people offer their assistance. These hungry souls will gratefully accept your help, as they are desperately looking for healthy masculine or feminine love. You will learn so much about your own child when you listen to your mentee's story, and you will bless him or her with your love. It is a win-win situation.

I've heard some wonderful stories of transformation through mentoring. Here are a few that may encourage you.

Sam Finds Help in the Military

I was either insane, trusting or being driven by God to talk to Sarge. He was a three-tour Army vet, complete with a Purple Heart and other medals. I had completed one tour. We were in Virginia. I was going through school, and he was one of the instructors.

I'd gotten to know Sarge because I was being selected to stay on and attend school and become an Army instructor for parachute rigging. I could sew well, and I was a meticulous packer. I was also attracted to other men but had been keeping away from gay bars and sexual association on the advice of a therapist I was seeing prior to being drafted into the Army. I had been an active homosexual from the age of fourteen until I was drafted at nineteen.

I was on an airplane back to Seattle from San Francisco. I had been there because on my seventeenth birthday when I told my mom I was gay, she sent me, as a gift, to live with three gay men she knew in San Francisco. I had a great time there, but on the plane trip back I was seized with the question, "Why am I queer?"

I spent time reading Freud, Adler, B. F. Skinner and others and began to understand some of the issues. This was 1967, so psychologists didn't encourage one to experiment and accept the feelings. I met with one therapist who started working with me, and then I was drafted.

The Army was good for me. When asked if I was a homosexual, I said no. And through boot camp, Ranger school and even in-country, I was following the advice of my therapist. I still had feelings for men from time to time, but the urges seemed under control.

And then there I was, sitting outside a packing shed with this sergeant, and I started telling him how I felt about men. That I was attracted to them, that I had a dad who ignored me and a stepfather who terrorized me and an uncle who locked me in a closet and on and on. Why did I trust him? God knows. But there I was. And when I finished and was getting up to run away, he said, "Ya know something, Son? Y'all ain't queer. You just need a real daddy."

"Yeah, right," I said.

"No, y'all needs someone to show you howse to be a man."

"I am a man," I responded.

"Well, ya sort of are. You're part way there. . . . Y'all come over for dinner. This ain't no place to talk, all right?"

So I went to dinner at his home. He and his wife said grace. I didn't believe in any god, as my parents were atheists and so I had grown up without a divine influence, albeit a fairly moral one. My father was an objectivist—Ayn Rand's philosophy.

After dinner the Sarge and I sat outside and we started talking. He just pretty much listened without judgment or comment. "Y'all need to come over here on Saturday and help me."

"Doing what?" I asked.

"I build birdhouses for the church sales, and I need you to cut wood and paint. By the way, ya know there ain't no queer deer, don't ya?"

"What?"

"God didn't make no queer deer. Takes two to make babies."

"Okay . . ."

"A man needs to know that he's responsible for his family, needs to have a family in order to become more of a man. . . . Any of your homosexual friends grownups? You ain't got to answer now. I just want you to think about it. . . . See you for dinner on Saturday. Bring your manners with you."

And this started a routine of me coming over for Saturday dinners as well as Friday nights. Sarge used to tell me, "Y'all git them feelings for a man, you come to the house. We'll just talk, and I'll put you to cutting wood and painting, and we'll have a beer." When I asked why a Southern Baptist had beer in the house, he said, "Well, Son, I don't hide it from the Lord. I don't get drunk. I like a cold beer now and then, and if I know a fellah's got a problem with his licker, then I offer him lemonade."

Sarge taught me how to fish and how to make birdhouses. His wife taught me how to make buttermilk biscuits and how to be a man toward women. I was always invited to church socials and to services on Sunday. Sometimes I went, but I was not convinced.

Sarge helped me get my license for parachute rigging and introduced me to skydiving. He took me hunting with other vets and showed me how to whittle a bit. He never told anyone that I was struggling, but he'd ask me how I was doing with my feelings.

"Y'all gettin' better these days. I see you lookin' at the cute forklift driver the other day."

"Her name is Susan," I said.

"You think she's pretty?" asked Sarge.

"Beautiful red hair, green eyes, and shapely too," I reported.

Sarge replied, "You sure you used to like boys? You startin' to sound like a lusty fellow to me!"

"I seem to be thinking that from time to time," I said.

"Well, you know there's a proper time for all that sex, don't you?"

"Yeah, yeah. Mrs. B told me it waits till marriage."

"God says so too. And though I know you ain't one to talk much about God, I want you to think about him. I'd like you to know him personally too. I got some books for you, cuz I know you're a thinker." He'd bought some books by Francis Schaeffer and C. S. Lewis for me, and a Bible with lots of ribbons in it marking passages. These were my birthday presents from him and his wife. "You got some reading to do." I put the books away.

I spent almost two years going to see Sarge, building birdhouses, talking, fishing, going out into the woods for one reason or another. We played catch, roughhoused and went shooting. Basically I found a dad I could love. When I left for school, he asked about the books. I promised I'd read them. I did. It would be years later before I became a Christian. But I'd stopped having sexual attractions for other men. I knew he and his wife had prayed many a prayer over me. He used to hug me and kissed me on the cheek on the rare occasion.

As far as I know, only he and his wife knew of my struggle. They did what no one had done before: loved me, listened to me, helped me as I struggled and provided for me a stable home and a steady diet of love. I also learned that a man could do many things like cook, sew and paint and still be a man of character with leadership qualities.

Sergeant Balderidge died about twenty years ago, and his wife followed shortly thereafter. But he had pictures of me, my wife and my son on his piano at home. To him, I was his son.

Bonnie Mentors Bonnie

Yes, they both have the same name. The Bonnie who did the mentoring has a son living a homosexual lifestyle. Here, in her words, are the lessons she learned while assisting a young woman with SSA named Bonnie in her healing process.[3]

As I recollect my journey as a mother of a homosexual son, time seems so indefinite. It seems like only yesterday that Matt shocked me with the revelation of his attraction to men. Yet as I ponder the experiences of the past fourteen years, it feels like I have survived a lifetime on an emotional roller coaster. The initial shock, heartache, depression, shattered dreams, hopelessness, grief and loneliness have all been interwoven in my mind and heart since I accepted the reality of our son's emotional brokenness.

Through the years, my husband and I have attended many support groups, conferences and seminars to educate ourselves as to the roots of homosexuality. We were also encouraged to love our child regardless of the inevitable changes in our relationship with him. He suddenly seemed like a different person from the one we had loved for so many years. There is an intense feeling of grief, as painful as the loss of a loved one due to death. Yet there are few sympathetic mourners and no sympathy cards. It made it a very lonely grieving process.

Years into the journey of loving our son while not approving of his sexual choices, I had another opportunity to understand the underlying damaged emotions of a person caught in the cycle of same-sex attractions. I received a phone call from a complete stranger who responded to an advertisement I'd put in a local paper concerning a support group for parents of gay children. My phone was the contact number for the group. When the call came, a woman asked my opinion concerning the healing of same-sex attraction. Did I consider the problem genetically based or a changeable emotional deficit? When

---

[3]The testimony of transformation of the Bonnie with SSA is in chapter eleven of *Coming Out Straight*.

I assured her that I knew about the process of reclaiming sexual wholeness, she was so relieved and hopeful.

We arranged to meet for lunch to get acquainted. The result is the story of God's plan whereby a person is able to comfort and act as a mentor in the life of a hurting, confused and vulnerable person.

We visited with each other and became friends who had a deep, controversial issue in common. Much of our time included intense discussions concerning the root issues of her lesbian feelings. I soon began to observe that this woman seriously wanted freedom from her unhealthy feelings toward other women.

She began to share about many of her wounds that began in childhood. Her inability to bond with an abusive mother, sexual abuse, an apathetic father and low self-esteem were all part of her ongoing problem of sexual distortion. As she continued to disclose her deep-seated feelings, I felt that she was begging for help in her healing process.

One day, while talking, she suggested to me an idea she had been considering for some time. She felt that if she could regain that lost mothering of her childhood then it might be a solid step toward restoration in her life.

I was familiar with Richard Cohen and his work on mentoring. We ordered his book *Healing Homosexuality: A New Treatment Plan* and his *Manual for Mentoring*.[4] Mentoring is a relational situation where the parent-child relationship is the basis of deep healing. We studied the book and spent time in prayer. I agreed to try to be her mentor. I called Richard, and we went for a session with him to fine-tune what we were doing. The woman I wanted to help had a lot of concerns about how to handle sexual feelings that might come up, among other things. Richard was available to us as we worked together, and at times we called for further help and encouragement.

---

[4]The contents of these are now part of *Coming Out Straight*.

In a nutshell, I became the mother that she did not have in child-hood. There were times of emotional upheaval when Bonnie age-regressed to childhood when sexual feelings for the mentor began to erupt. The sessions were never the same, but an abundance of tears were shed. Sometimes our times were easy, more enlightening and less emotional. When we had more intense sessions, I needed time to digest areas that were new and hard for me to deal with, like sex-ual abuse, promiscuity and her many unmet needs. Through this course, I became much more compassionate toward both survivors of sexual abuse and emotionally disturbed adults.

I recommend this mentoring relationship to a sexually secure adult who wants to reach out to help broken people in the area of sexual identity. It requires a commitment of time and emotional support. Without a doubt, I was entrusted with the opportunity to make a dif-ference in the life of a person who struggled with the homo-emotional issue. I was unable to help my own son, so I thought, *Why not offer motherhood to a "spiritual daughter" whose root issues closely match those of my son?*

There is a real need for mentors. Few people are willing to commit and travel through the garbage and pain. It is not fun or pleasant. However, there were many occasions during the process when I knew how much I was needed and how much the adult child appre-ciated my love. This balances the scale and provides the blessings along the way. I feel valuable as a person who, through time, love and trust, was able to be a life-changing source for someone else.

I especially urge parents of homosexual children to enter into this life-giving experience with a person who wants to end the battle with homo-emotional feelings. We often cannot heal our own children. Why not use the time we might spend lamenting over our son or daughter to provide a healing relationship for another broken child?

Conclusion

At the beginning of this book I wrote about my son, Jarish, and the struggles he went through as a teenager. He was deeply hurt by me in the earliest years of his life. As I struggled with my own SSA, I put my wife and children through hell because of my anger, pain and unavailability. My son's detachment was a result of my behavior and the tremendous conflict between my wife and me.

After I went through my own healing journey and finally "came out straight," Jae Sook and I worked passionately to restore our own relationship and then to reconcile with the kids. But by then Jarish had built many walls around his heart. As we tried to reach him, Jae Sook and I cried many tears together. It was not easy for us to see him go through so much unnecessary pain. It broke our hearts. But we never stopped loving him, and we prayed without ceasing. We fought with him, did family healing sessions, did anything we could to move his heart.

Finally, in his junior year at college in England, God knocked on his door and Jarish listened. In that moment his heart was circumcised and he fell to his knees in repentance. He realized what he had done was wrong and cried out to God for forgiveness. Once again, he began to study God's Word voraciously.

It was a dream come true, a miracle that God had given to us all. But it did not happen overnight or without effort. It took years of tears, prayers, investment and perseverance to win him back. We used all the tools described in this book. Today our son has come "home," and he is following God. For this we are eternally grateful.

I held my son hundreds of times while he was growing up. I said "I love you" thousands of times. But once the walls went up, those positive memories were gone with the wind. It is true for all parents: too much pain inside our children keeps them from receiving whatever good we have to give. That is why it is critical to break through with each one of them, regardless of the issues they are dealing with.

Our son did not have SSA, but with a few exceptions, the process of reaching him and offering healing was nearly identical with the process I've described in the pages of this book. SSA or not, we were dealing with our son's pain and his living a lifestyle we had never wanted for him. The presenting issues may be different, but the solution is always the same: love God with all your heart, love yourself as you are loved and love others. And love without ceasing.

Jarish wrote part of his life story for his youth group. I asked his permission to share it with you.

I was born into an atmosphere that no child wishes to be brought into; but alas, the past cannot be physically altered. My father was still a child inside (that is, emotionally, as most people in this world tend to be), as was my mother. He was struggling with a most grave problem: that of homosexuality. You may take it lightly, not being able to relate to it, but the reality is that he endured unfathomable pain and suffering in his heart and soul. And my mother was like a scared little girl. She was placed in an orphanage for a year when she was seven while her parents went off to do mission work in Korea back in the 1960s. It scarred her for life.

I cannot recall the first point of detachment from my parents. All I know is that it happened, as it happens to so many of us, whether we know it or not and whether our parents know it or not. We conceal it from our parents. We give them the fake smiles, the fake love. Outwardly we are happy, but inside there is a voice of a child screaming, "I hate your guts! Be the father or mother you are supposed to be!" My father continuously worked on healing his heart, and my parents' relationship began to mend. Meanwhile I continued to grow more numb to their love.

The weight of my hatred lay more with my father than my mother. On the one hand, I respected my father as someone who was doing more for God and the world than I saw any other man doing. Yes, there was a pride within me that *he,* this individual, was my father. However, there also lay within my heart another feeling toward this man. This concerned his role as a father. I hated his guts as a father. He was a great individual for the world, but a horrible father for me, and more often than not, I hated him because of it. I could not bypass my feelings of anger and resentment, for I wanted him to be a father to me more than I wanted him to be a man who saved the world. A father who loves his son, I believe, in reality saves the world by saving his son's life. And this love is irreplaceable.

I really started to fall away from my family in high school. I was so weak inside, so vulnerable to a world that is consumed with temporary fixes, temporary happiness and temporary love. Life had no meaning. Disillusionment resided within me. Life was just a means to a sad, horrible end, I figured. Emptiness is a horrible feeling. I wanted to die so badly. The relationship with my parents grew more and more superficial every day. When my father would ask me what I felt, I would say, "I feel nothing." Translation: I am a numb, spiritually dead individual who cannot get in touch with himself. When you become that numb inside, feeling is but a luxury.

So, I took to the bottle. Alcohol, I loved alcohol. It made me *feel* something. I could escape my present reality and enter a world where I could act out all the indiscretions stuffed deep inside my heart. I felt happy, but soon I would return to that dull, empty baseline feeling the next morning (not to mention some wicked hangovers). I got involved with girls. I was searching for love. I could *feel* there too. No matter how much I convinced myself that this was true love, though, deep down inside I knew it wasn't. I was trying to compensate for something I was dearly lacking. But no matter how hard I tried, I could not fill my heart with what it was I wanted so badly.

I really wanted to die. I would often ask God to send a car flying into mine so maybe it would have been an accident that I died. I remember sitting on the edge of a cliff, looking at the rocks below, and thinking to myself, *Wouldn't it be wonderful if someone could come along and push me off? Let this miserable life end.* The fact of the matter was, my parents had been getting better the whole time and were trying to love me, but I could not feel it, partly because I was detached and partly because I had made an internal decision not to receive them into my life. I was hurt and wounded.

This progressed until I left to study abroad for a semester in England during my junior year in college. That is when my life was turned around. I woke up out of a deep slumber. It was as if someone had put defibrillators to my soul, cranked up the juice and pumped a thousand volts through me. I took a step back from all the girls, alcohol, partying and all the other meaningless crap that consumed my life and looked at myself. What I saw horrified me and touched me all at once: the endless cycle of trying to find happiness and love, but never being able to get ahold of it. Highs and lows. That's all it was. I realized, *Why not feel happy all the time?* I had searched to feel satisfaction and fulfillment in almost every avenue possible. There was only one answer that resounded in my heart and soul. The beginning was the end. I had to come full circle. My family, my parents, were the only answer.

I began talking to my parents more about my life, God and Scripture. I became closer to them than I had ever been, and I was three thousand miles away! A great ocean can divide a son from his father and mother, but love can bridge even that expanse. I couldn't wait to come home. I just rushed into my parents' arms. I returned home a new person. I confessed all my wrongdoings to them, and I cried and cried with them. I was that little boy again, receiving the love that wasn't available before.

One hundred eighty degrees. That's what happened to me. But life isn't always so cut and dry. One still has to deal with all the pain and hurt. I must say that even after I had reformed myself, guilt rained down on me. Days would pass, and I would think of how bad a person I was. But it was my father and mother who truly liberated my heart. It took one comment from my dad to take away all my worries and guilt: "God doesn't accuse. Satan accuses." And I then realized how true his explanation was. It's like that scene in *Good Will Hunting* when the therapist (Robin Williams), as a last resort, keeps saying to Will (Matt Damon), "It's not your fault, Will . . . it's not your fault . . . it's not your fault." That's how it felt. And I cried and cried, realizing that God was not accusing me—he was embracing me.

In reconnecting with my parents I did and still do practice some healing techniques. Back when I was in high school, our family had a session with a therapist who introduced the concept of "holding" and "attachment" work. This might sound out of the ordinary to you, or just bizarre. And mind you, it was the first couple of times. But the overall concept makes sense. My parents would hold me and just kiss my face until I'd crack and ask them to stop it. One can get extremely frustrated by this repeated action. It's like Chinese water torture, but a lot more intimate. Of course, me, being the cocky fifteen- or sixteen-year-old I was at that time, thought that I would ignore it all and could withstand it. Believe me, you have to be dead to withstand this type of therapy. Anyway, I definitely cracked, and out poured all of the sickness inside of me. Of course I didn't like the whole affair one bit, as I was still struggling to find myself and my worth in this world.

These days, though, I willingly accept holding from my parents, because it feels good to release all the pain, anger and resentment stuffed inside for all those years. It's okay to be angry with your parents. It's okay to be resentful, because you are just a hurt child deep down inside who never received the warm love and affection you needed.

All children deserve 100 percent pure love. We deserve ideal parents. You cannot grow internally, emotionally, spiritually, without *receiving* love from your parents or parental figures. It's like there's an emotional cancer within every one of us, and we need to get it out. In addition to holding, I also just pound and yell into a pillow when I'm angry. This helps me release a lot of that pent-up anger and hurt. When I say, "Dad, Dad, Dad," over and over again and recount the images of him not being there for me or yelling at me or hurting me, then the pain and hurt comes out naturally. At the end of it all, I feel loved, I feel good. I feel a sense of worth.

When my father puts his arms around me and holds me and I just cry and cry, it's what I always wanted deep down inside, no matter how much I tried to deny it. All I wanted was my father and mother to hold me and tell me they loved me and tell me how good a person I am. That is what every child wants, and it's because we grow up as wounded children (most of us) that we are reluctant to agree to such love, or we feel uncomfortable in the situations I just described. But the truth is, deep down inside it is what we are all longing for.

My desires for the temporary fixes of this world melt away when I receive this type of love. And as I continue to heal my heart, they dissipate more and more. For as my dad says, "Healing is not a destination, it is a process." It takes a lot of work to heal one's heart, but I want it so badly so that I can become a better person for me, for God and for my wife.

My parents were truly God-like during the whole period of my inner turmoil. They set boundaries for my actions but did not directly interfere in my life. They only stood by me and offered me the most precious thing they had: their unconditional love. My dad once told me, "Jarish, I know we give you gifts, money, but it's all meaningless compared with the greatest gift we can give you, and that is love and healing in your life." How right he is.

Now you must seriously ask yourself what or who is your rock? What is it that you can fall back on when you are in the pits of hell? My rock is my parents. They have always stood by my side, no matter how many times I damned them. My relationship with God soared because I felt the presence of God in my parents and through my parents. A key point to this is that my parents were willing to change for me. They were willing to do anything to melt my heart because they felt pained to see me so pained. I am a reflection of them, and when the son hurts, the father and mother also hurt.

These days when I see my father, I feel so much of God through him. He is doing awesome things for God in this world. He is a great individual for this world. And finally, what I respect and cherish even more than that is that he is a great father to me! I can finally say that the love felt between us is indescribable. It transcends life itself. I finally have a father who will hold me, who will tell me he loves me, who will tell me I am worth something, who will get down on one knee and tearfully repent to his son for all the heartache that he has caused him in his life. Do you know how that feels? To have a parent who will ask for forgiveness, even though much of the pain he caused he couldn't help. That is when the word *parent* actually has meaning behind it. That's when a parent actually becomes a real parent, a true parent.

As I write these words, they come very slowly and painfully. Tears run down my face, as I cannot contain the feelings and images that have shaped my life. It hurts when you are not loved, do not feel loved or accepted. I see my former self: hurt, broken, struggling to find love, happiness. I see my present self: so beautiful, healing every day, restoring everything that had been broken—pulling weeds and planting seeds within my soul and psyche. I see my future self: perfect, happy, loved, giving love. I am a good person. I am God's precious child. I finally feel loved. I truly feel it. It's as if all of heaven and earth could pass away but I would still be alive because God and true love reside within me![1]

Final Comments

Now that you have read this book, I hope you will go back and read it again, and again if necessary, until you are certain that SSA is essentially not about sex and that this is truly a battle of love. *And whoever loves the most and longest wins!* Keep rereading until you know in your heart of hearts that there is much you can do to promote positive changes in your child's life and in the lives of your family members, friends and community of faith.

And remember, the man who wrote this book was once totally and completely homosexually oriented. Today I am totally and completely heterosexually oriented. It took many years and tears, but I stand as a man among men. And so can your son. And so can your daughter be a woman among women.

Now that you know what to do, please continue without ceasing. *I suggest that you write a personalized treatment plan based on the twelve steps.* Make both short- and long-range goals. Map it out. Those who take the time to write out their goals have a much greater success rate than those who do not. After you finish writing your treatment plan, take time to share it with your spouse. Support each other's plan. Make it a team effort. (See the appendix for sample treatment plans created by parents in our teleconferencing classes.)

Remember, *you must be real and feel in order to heal.* The more you become transparent and vulnerable with your child, the more he will open up to you. Change will occur for everyone involved in the healing process. How you apply the treatment plan will depend on your child's age and whether he lives at home or on his own. If your child lives at home,

---

[1] Jarish is now working on his M.D./Ph.D. and plans to do cancer research. His wife is a pre-med student at the same university. They are doing beautifully. We all thank God.

work diligently to create secure attachment before he leaves. You have a marvelous opportunity to turn this around. If your child lives away from home, you must be more creative in your efforts. Whatever the situation, love is spelled Time, Touch and Talk.

When you first begin to utilize these skills to create greater intimacy with your SSA child, you may feel like you are failing. That is natural. Stick to the program and eventually you will work your way back into his heart.

The keys to healing same-sex attraction are (1) understanding the truth of SSA, (2) asking forgiveness for mistakes and making restitution, and (3) loving ceaselessly and correctly. The "innate, immutable" mythology of homosexuality is one of the greatest hoaxes ever pulled off in human history. It was a well-conceived and well-executed strategy to stop prejudice toward homosexually oriented men and women. Why? Because the church, mental health profession, social institutions and families failed to understand and properly love these men and women. We are now paying for these sins.

God has chosen you to rectify these failures through the immediacy of your own child's struggle. As painful as this fact is, you have been selected to end this cultural war by unconditionally loving your child. Use this plan. Take it slowly. Set small goals at first. *Succeed small rather than fail big.* Succeed in one or two things, and then add more steps to accomplish. Feel good about yourself and your child in the process.

What I have learned in my own journey of healing is that it is all about the process, not the results. Be in the moment. Appreciate your child today, and don't withhold your affection as you wait for him to "change." Change comes ever so slowly, sometimes unnoticeably. It is in the loving that we are transformed. Remember once again: *This is a marathon, not a sprint.* Keep breathing, praying, laughing and crying, and pace yourself. Experience as much love as possible, so you can give from abundance, not out of guilt and fear.

One father in a teleconferencing class said, "It's all about love, being vulnerable, honest, transparent and seeing into the heart of your child." To do that, you will have to face yourself, over and over again. *Through helping your child heal, you too will be transformed.*

If you need your child or loved one to change, most likely she will not. If you don't need her to change, more likely she will. Accept and love her as she is right now. Do your best and God will do the rest.

You *can* get your child back. You may lose many battles, but ultimately, with the power of God's love and mercy, and the help of many family members and friends, you will win them back. Hang in there, Mom and Dad. The story is not over yet. Remember, love is the strongest medicine to heal all pain.

The following are several treatment plans created by parents who have participated in International Healing Foundation teleconferencing classes. All names have been changed, and the plans are used with permission.

John's Treatment Plan

Objective: To create and maintain closeness and secure attachment with Robert.

STEP ONE: Deal with my emotions and thoughts about Robert's SSA.

  1. **Goal:** Calm my gut reactions.

    Task: When I have a bad thought or reaction about SSA, think of the love my son needs.

    Complete by: Ongoing.

    Notes: This is a helpful tool to remind me how I should learn to feel and then react. This has already helped me several times at work.

  2. **Goal:** Become "counterintuitive."

    Task: Before saying or doing anything, think "counterintuitive."

    Complete by: Ongoing.

  3. **Goal:** Stay positive.

    Task: Read uplifting, encouraging articles and books.

    Complete by: Ongoing.

STEP TWO: Take care of myself.

> **Goal:** Get help from church family.
>
> **Task:** Meet with the two youth pastors to discuss Robert's situation.
>
> Complete by: May 28.
>
> Notes: Meeting set for May 27.

STEP THREE: Go to God. Experience God.

> 1. **Goal:** Give it to God.
>
> **Task:** Pray about this *daily!* Help me understand the reasons for his SSA, and show me how I can help heal my son. Give me the strength daily.
>
> Complete by: Ongoing, daily.
>
> Notes: It is always a great relief to give things over to God!
>
> 2. **Goal:** Visualize Robert healed.
>
> **Task:** When praying, remember to think of him as healed and fulfilling his destiny.
>
> Complete by: Ongoing.

STEP FOUR: Investigate the causes and treatment of SSA.

> 1. **Goal:** Read literature.
>
> **Task:** Reread chapter two of *Coming Out Straight.*
>
> Complete by: May 23.
>
> 2. **Goal:** Research about peer wounds.
>
> Complete by: June 15.

STEP SIX: Make things right between Robert and me.

> 1. **Goal:** Spend as much time as possible together this holiday weekend. Talk and share.

2. Make an affirmation tape and write a letter.

   Task: Finish the letter I started a couple months ago.

   Complete by: June 30.

   Task: Record a CD of positive affirmations.

   Complete by: July 16.

STEP SEVEN: Investigate Robert's love language.

1. **Goal:** Define Robert's primary love language and then give it to him.

   Task: Finished *The Five Love Languages* in April.

   Notes: His primary love languages are physical touch and acts of service. Keep practicing those and remember to give him all five too!

   Task: Touch and hug him as much as possible. Remember to practice all five!

2. **Goal:** Do things he likes.

   Task: Took him to a music concert.

   Notes: Had a great time together, lots of fun.

3. **Goal:** Share in activities.

   Task: Possible trip to California (peer friends there too).

   Task: Record some music together. Take a few days off work in June to do some music together.

   Task: Try to get him to work out with me.

STEP EIGHT: Display appropriate physical affection.

1. **Goal:** Touch, bless and love.

   Task: Hug, kiss and bless Robert each day. Tell him I love him.

   Complete by: Ongoing.

Notes: This has really been effective. Even getting hugs back now.

May 15 update: He has pulled back this week because he is mad that I am hugging his boyfriend too. Don't stop! Keep it up!

STEP ELEVEN: Friends and acquaintances.

1. **Goal:** Meet and get to know his friends.

    Task: Invite them over for a barbecue, watch a movie, soak in the hot tub.

    Complete by: Ongoing.

    Notes: They came over for pizza on Friday. Keep inviting.

    Task: Try to get them over for a sleepover this weekend.

2. **Goal:** Love and show affection to his boyfriend.

    Task: Hug him every time I see him.

    Complete by: Ongoing.

    Notes: He really responds positively to my affection, but it has upset Robert!

STEP TWELVE: Same-sex mentors.

1. **Goal:** Find mentors for Robert.

    Task: Build a support network.

    Task: Get older cousins involved. Continue the "guys night out."

    Task: If youth pastors seem supportive, encourage Robert to go to some summer activities.

As you can see, John mentioned many of the steps but left some out. He chose to focus on these at this time.

Anne's Treatment Plan (John's Wife)

STEP ONE: Deal with my emotions and thoughts about Robert's SSA.

1. Journaling: Write down my emotions, thoughts and feelings whenever I'm feeling depressed or overwhelmed.

   (This is ongoing—started a few months ago.)

2. Educating myself: Create a library of books regarding SSA.

   Visiting websites recommended by Richard.

   (This is ongoing—started months ago.)

3. Pray.

4. Set aside one hour a day as "my time" for reading, exercise, a nap or prayer.

   (Alert children—starts June 2.)

5. Create a support group (my mom, sister, brothers and Sarah). Share with them what Richard is teaching us, his book and websites that will help educate them about SSA. Ask them to pray with me on specific situations as they arise.

   (Finish creating support group by week's end—June 6 or 7.)

STEP TWO: Make things right between me and my husband.

1. Start our Friday-night dates again.

   (Starting this Friday—ongoing.)

2. Practice communication techniques.

   (Starting this Friday on date nights—ongoing.)

3. Pray together.

   (Every night starting now—ongoing.)

STEP THREE: Go to God. Experience love.

1. Spend daily time with God in prayer and in his Word.

   Praying for wisdom and strength. Praying to be John's support while keeping my mouth closed.

(Ongoing.)

2. Continue Monday-night Bible study with the women at church and ask for prayer and support for Robert.

(Starts June 14—ongoing.)

STEP FOUR: Investigate the causes and treatment of SSA.

1. Create a library based on the books recommended by Richard.

(Began months ago—ongoing.)

2. Investigate Robert's love language.

(Done—Robert's language is physical touch.)

These are the first four steps of many. I would like to work on these first before moving on.

Jessica's Treatment Plan

1. I plan to take care of myself by continuing to run and swim and lift weights four times per week. I will continue my daily devotions and lift up the memories of Patrick's childhood that alarmed or frightened me using Flora Slosson Wuellner's book *Prayer, Stress and My Inner Wounds.* Her chapters called "With Christ to the Painful Past" and "With Christ to Deep Forgotten Pain" will also aid me in lifting up some of my painful memories and present anger toward my separation from my parents. Richard Cohen's thought: "Your child may be carrying some of your unhealed wounds and unmet needs, or the unhealed wounds and unmet needs of the lineage," is my inspiration, for the probability is great. I will try to figure out what my emotional and physical needs are and ask my husband [Alan] and others to help meet them. I will initiate this conversation by taking my husband's hand and telling him what I think my needs are and if it feels like they are not being met. I will ask him if he can help me meet these needs. If it doesn't happen in

a healthy way, I will reconcile with him, trusting in the grace and forgiveness of Christ in our relationship. I will seek professional help if necessary.

2. I have asked support from two very close prayerful friends and from two pastors. They are very supportive and faithful in praying the following specific prayers:

     a. Healing God, please help Patrick's family to grow closer to you and to one another. May Patrick know God's powerful love through Alan's love and strong attention in these days before leaving for the summer, and forever after.

     b. Healing God, help Patrick to understand why he is attracted to the same sex, and give him a desire to feel at home in his heart, mind and body.

     c. Healing God, melt the wall of shame and loneliness around Patrick's heart, that he might begin to embrace his masculinity and find peace and power in it, as God intended.

     d. Healing God, bring Alan and Jessica [their daughter], her husband, and Patrick together for the Family Healing Session, so that they might leave the baggage from the past and begin to seek a reconciled relationship in all the days of their future. [We had a Family Healing Session, and remarkable breakthroughs occurred.]

3. I will support Alan by asking him how I can help, by encouraging him and, most important, by asking God to help me know when to ask or suggest and when to keep quiet. Since Alan is also praying this prayer in an effort to strategize together to love Patrick, I will accept when he does not do what I suggest. Daily, I will pray, "Creator of Patrick, You love him even more than we do. Please help him feel your unconditional love, and may he know the heal-

ing power of your love." I will also suggest time away for Alan and me; and we will strive to keep our Friday-night dinner-and-dancing-at-home date.

4. I will write a letter to Patrick expressing my regrets and mail this to him this summer. I know about his fear of feeling abandoned, so I will apologize to him for those times and ask his forgiveness. I will also tell him about the times when I was alarmed or afraid that he was "born a homosexual," and I will tell him why. I will say, "I am sorry for the pain I caused you in my ignorance and confusion and denial."

5. I will read *The Five Love Languages of Teenagers* and *Growing Up Straight* by the end of the summer, so I can gain knowledge and be encouraged. I will log on to NARTH, PeopleCanChange and other websites and read articles when I am discouraged.

6. I will affirm Patrick's dad in front of Patrick at least once a day in their presence. I will pray for same-sex mentors and friends for Patrick; this will be a passionate and persistent prayer, as he is away this summer. I will ask God to provide at least one male friend who does not wish to have sex with him, that he might discover what it means to be accepted and loved by a true friend of the same sex. "Lord, have mercy."

7. By June 20, I will write a letter to my parents, expressing my regrets at our distant relationship, and in particular I will express my anger and pain over the use of "the code" to reach them. I will express my regrets that they did not take a stronger interest in our children or in what I do in life. I will also include gratitude for the gifts and treasures that they gave to me as a child and adolescent.

This is my short-range treatment plan. It strikes me that many of the goals can be carried over into the next few years, but during that time I will specifically pray that Patrick will know of God's love and power in his life, know of God's good intention for a fulfilling life with a wonderful woman, know healing in his heart, mind and body, and sustain and be able to nurture relationships with the same sex that have nothing to do with sex.

God can work miracles, and I believe that our meeting Richard was divine intervention and timing. If Patrick begins to know God's love through Alan, and through me taking a backseat in his life, as hard as it is, and if he begins to bond with same-sex peers, understanding that he is a beautiful male creation of God's grand design and if he doesn't experiment with a sexual relationship with a peer, then it may be possible for him to go to college next year. But I will be praying for guidance and discernment while he is away this summer. And Alan and I will be working on inviting important adult male mentors to be an essential part of his life when he returns.

Patrick went away to school, found a remarkable group of male friends and is on his own path of healing. He himself said, "The gay life is not for me."

Jim's Treatment Plan

This is a list of steps for my action plan (both short and long term) for my relationship with Tony. [Note: If no specific time frame is expressed, the item reflects both short- and long-term goals.]

1. Deal with emotions.

   - Continue to focus on the fifth stage of grieving (acceptance) to ensure that I'm focusing on what I can do to assist Tony in this process.

2. Take care of myself.

   - Continue to keep God as a primary focus in my life and to make him an integral part of getting us all through this and never lose faith. To see and have faith in God's completed work at the end.

- Continue to support my wife, Debby, and Tony throughout this process, to not solve their problems but instead listen and console.

3. Get support.

- Find others to broaden prayer support for Tony and our family.

4. Make things right between Debby and me.

- Listen to Debby and her concerns.

- Continue to tell Debby that she did nothing wrong, that she was filling a void that I left in my relationship with Tony.

- Continue to love and support Debby and let Tony see that we are committed as a couple to love and uplift him.

5. Go to God.

- Continue to make God an integral part of my daily life. Ask him for his wisdom to know what to do and his grace to do it.

- Be more aware of the opportunities God may present to learn about what I need to do and ways to help Tony and others in overcoming SSA.

6. Make things right with my SSA child.

- Short term: Finish the corrections on my letter to Tony, and let Richard review it.

- Short term: Find time to ask Tony how he felt when I did not take immediate action on doing something for him when he initially told me about his SSA. After listening, try to explain the dilemma I had with Debby being very stressed out with her job, my being out of work and our running very low on money. Need to stress that it wasn't that I didn't care but that I was very concerned about Mom being pushed over the edge with everything we had going on at that point.

- Long term: Share my letter with Tony.

- Find other opportunities to share my feelings about things that have happened to me, to let Tony know I can identify with the struggles he is going through and how emotionally difficult it must be. Let him know that he is not alone and give him hope that he can get through this and possibly be stronger and better for it.

7. Investigate the causes of SSA.

- Spend more time finding and reading materials on both sides of the SSA issue.

- Read literature to better understand Tony and his SSA.

8. Learn Tony's love language.

- Reread *The Five Love Languages*.

- Especially pay close attention to the section on Tony's love language: quality time.

- Continue to find opportunities to make special time with Tony and his friends and family.

- Continue to tell and show Tony how very special and important he is to us.

9. Exchange literature.

- Find out where Tony is at concerning information on the gay brochures, and see if there is anything else he wants me to read or do.

10. Discover Tony's interests.

- I know Tony's biggest interests are cars, houses and currently finding another dog.

- I need to continue to find ways to help him focus in these areas.

- Since Tony is currently out of work, we are going to subscribe to every car magazine he likes, to have him reading this instead of being tempted by Internet pornography.

- We have given Tony a green light to get a dog that he wants, to hopefully fill the void of love he needs while we are all working on his recovery. He knows that a dog in the house is the last thing we were looking for. We also want him to know that we know how important this is to him and we are making real efforts to be there for him and to do what is best for his well-being.

11. Work on communication skills.

- Reread Richard's notes on reflective listening.

- Find opportunities to engage Tony on different things that have happened to him in his past and practice these skills to create a closer relationship with him.

12. Make an affirmation tape.

- Short term: Ask Richard the best way to approach Tony about giving him the tape once it is completed.

- Create an outline of areas I should be covering on the tape.

- Put down the details of these areas and create the tape.

13. Be affectionate.

- Continue to display appropriate affection toward Tony and let him know how very special he is to me.

14. Get to know his friends.

- Continue to ask about and meet his friends and inquire about who he is going out with.

- Create opportunities to meet his friends, and possibly arrange cookouts.

15. Pray.

- Make a more concerted effort to be more specific in things I need help on from God and my prayer requests to God.

- Continue to see Tony healed with a great loving wife and three beautiful children. See him being a great dad and having a grateful heart for God's deliverance from his SSA.

16. Find other mentors.

- Make opportunities to have Tony's (healthy) guy friends be part of his life. Invite them to cookouts or dinner with us as a family.

- Include Tony in other activities that I'm involved in with other guys (friends or relatives).

17. Mentor others with SSA.

- Currently Tony does not indicate that he is hanging out with other SSA people. We have made an effort to meet other people he has told us about, but we're not 100 percent sure if they are SSA-related friends or not.

18. Do your own work.

- Find out more about healing activities and start approaching Tony about going together.

Recommended Reading List

General Books on Homosexuality

The Battle for Normality (Gerard van den Aardweg)

Coming Out Straight (Richard Cohen)

Desires in Conflict (Joe Dallas)

God's Grace and the Homosexual Next Door (Alan Chambers)

Homosexuality and the Politics of Truth (Jeffrey Satinover)

Homosexuality: A Freedom Too Far (Charles Socarides)

Homosexuality: A New Christian Ethic (Elizabeth Moberly)

Loving Homosexuals as Jesus Would (Chad Thompson)

My Genes Made Me Do It (Neil and Briar Whitehead)

101 Frequently Asked Questions About Homosexuality (Mike Haley)

One Man, One Woman, One Lifetime (Rabbi Rueven Bulka)

Striving for Gender Identity (Christl Ruth Vonholdt)

The Truth Comes Out (Nancy Heche)

You Don't Have to Be Gay (Jeff Konrad)

Books for Parents

Growing Up Straight (Peter and Barbara Wyden)

Healing Word, The (Cindy Rullman)

Ounce of Prevention (Don Schmierer)

A Parent's Guide to Preventing Homosexuality (Joseph and Linda Ames Nicolosi)

Someone I Love Is Gay (Bob Davies and Anita Worthen)

When Homosexuality Hits Home (Joe Dallas)

Where Does a Mother Go to Resign? (Barbara Johnson)

Male Homosexuality

Growth into Manhood (Alan Medinger)

Healing Homosexuality: Case Stories of Reparative Therapy (Joseph Nicolosi)

Practical Exercises for Men in Recovery of SSA (James Phelan)

Reparative Therapy of Male Homosexuality (Joseph Nicolosi)

Female Homosexuality

Born That Way? (Erin Eldridge)

Female Homosexuality: Choice Without Volition (Elaine Siegel)

Out of Egypt (Jeanette Howard)

Restoring Sexual Identity: Hope for Women Who Struggle with SSA (Anne Paulk)

Homosexual Movement and Activities

After the Ball (Marshall Kirk and Hunter Madsen)

Answers to the Gay Deception (Marlin Maddoux)

Homosexuality and American Psychiatry (Ronald Bayer)

"The Trojan Coach: How the Mental Health Guilds Allow Medical Diagnostics, Scientific Research and Jurisprudence to Be Subverted in Lockstep with the Political Aims of Their Gay Sub-Components" (Jeffrey Satinover, <www.narth.com>)

"Selling Homosexuality to America" (Paul Rondeau, *Law Review*, Regent University 14, no. 2 [Spring 2002]: 443-85)

Homosexual Behavior

Getting It Straight (Peter Sprigg and Timothy Dailey)

International Resources

Courage/Encourage

Telephone: (212) 268-1010

Web: www.couragerc.net

Catholic support groups for strugglers and family members. Fr. John Harvey, director.

Evergreen International

Telephone: (800) 391-1000

Web: www.evergreeninternational.org

Mormon support groups for strugglers and family members. David Pruden, director.

Exodus North America

Telephone: (407) 599-6872

Web: www.exodus.to

Umbrella organization for ex-gay Christian ministries. Alan Chambers, director.

Homosexual Anonymous

Telephone: (610) 779-2500

Web: www.ha-fs.org

Christian-based recovery groups for those with unwanted SSA. David E., director.

Inqueery

Web: www.inqueery.com

Addressing homosexuality in schools and colleges. Chad Thompson, director.

International Healing Foundation (IHF)

Telephone: (301) 805-6111

Web: www.comingoutstraight.com / www.gaychildrenstraightparents.com

Healing seminars, teleconferencing classes, counseling. Richard Cohen, executive director.

Jews Offering New Alternatives to Homosexuality (JONAH)

Telephone: (201) 433-3444

Web: www.jonahweb.org

Support for strugglers and family members. Arthur Goldberg and Elaine Berk, codirectors.

National Association for Research and Therapy of Homosexuality (NARTH)

Telephone: (818) 789-4440

Web: www.narth.com

Therapists assisting those with unwanted SSA. Joseph Nicolosi, president.

One by One

Telephone: (585) 586-6180

Web: www.oneby1.org

Ex-gay ministry for the Presbyterian Church. Kristin Johnson, executive director.

Parents and Friends of Ex-Gays and Gays (PFOX)

Telephone: (703) 360-2225

Web: www.pfox.org

Support for family members and friends. Regina Griggs, national director.

People Can Change

Web: www.peoplecanchange.com

Online support groups, healing retreats and stories of transformation. Rich Wyler, executive director.

Positive Alternatives to Homosexuality (PATH)

Web: www.pathinfo.org

International coalition for groups supporting change.

Powerful Change Ministry Group

Telephone: (770) 210-4034

Web: www.witnessfortheworld.org

African-American Ministries for those dealing with SSA. D. L. Foster, director.

Transforming Congregations

Telephone: (302) 945-9650

Web: www.transformingcong.org

Ex-gay ministry for the United Methodist Church. Karen Booth, director.

Other Websites

www.dawnstefanowicz.com (help for individuals whose parents are SSA)

www.healinghomosexuality.com (therapist Floyd Godfrey and Adventure in Manhood [AIM] website) www.janellehallman.com (female therapist helping women with un-wanted SSA)

www.becomingreal.org/articles/change.htm (research on the efficacy of change)

www.realityresources.com (transgender support in the United States)

Pro-Homosexual Websites

www.advocate.com (national gay and lesbian magazine *The Advocate*)

www.glsen.org (Gay Lesbian Straight Education Network)

www.hrc.org (Human Rights Campaign)

www.lambdalegal.org (Lambda Legal Defense Fund)

www.TheTaskForce.org (National Gay and Lesbian Task Force)

www.pflag.org (Parents and Friends of Lesbians and Gays)

Addendum

Healing Seminars and Family Healing Sessions

Healing Seminars

There are several excellent programs available for healing, whether one is dealing with individual, couple or family issues. These are experiential programs designed to help bring about personal and relational healing and transformation. Another benefit from attending such seminars is that you learn from one another and make lasting friends.

Adventure in Manhood (AIM)

Sponsored by Family Strategies, www.adventureinmanhood.com
This weekend focuses on helping men develop their gender esteem through masculine outdoor activity. Men participate with their father or a mentor who is supporting them in their journey out of SSA. The mission of AIM is to foster healthy bonding with men through masculine activity, teamwork and socialization. AIM challenges individuals physically, mentally and spiritually in a safe circle of healthy men.

Journey Into Manhood (JIM)

Sponsored by People Can Change, www.peoplecanchange.com
This weekend offers experiential exercises and inner-healing processes for men who are serious about working to overcome and resolve unwanted SSA. The retreat is designed to help attendees look at their inner perceptions, explore feelings about men and women, and gain a clearer vision for life. JIM is intended for men who want to lessen or eliminate homosexual desires and embrace heterosexual masculinity.

Love/Sex/Intimacy (LSI) Healing Seminars

Sponsored by the International Healing Foundation, www.ComingOut Straight.com

LSI Healing Seminars are held four to six times throughout the year. They are appropriate for all family members to attend. We also sponsor Father-Son and Mother-Daughter Healing Seminars. We have been facilitating these seminars for eighteen years throughout the United States and Europe, assisting thousands of men and women in their journey toward wholeness. This is an opportunity for everyone to share from their hearts and experience tremendous healing. We offer real and practical solutions for both personal and family issues. All are welcome.

New Warrior Training Adventure and Woman Within

Sponsored by The Mankind Project (www.mkp.org) and by Woman Within International (www.womanwithin.org) respectively

These weekends are open to all people and have no direct connection with the issue of homosexuality. However, it is important to know that they will support someone's choice to be "gay" or their choice to "change." This is an opportunity for mother and daughter or father and son to share a powerful, life-changing weekend (or your children may attend on their own). The benefit of these weekends is that they offer same gender support groups after the weekend. The men have I-groups (I=Integration) and the women have E-groups (E=Empowerment).

Family Healing Sessions

Sponsored by the International Healing Foundation, www.ComingOut Straight.com

You may also consider participating in family healing sessions. Some therapists are trained in family therapy and may facilitate this experience. I myself have worked with many families when a loved one is dealing with SSA, and it is astounding to see years of pain and resentment melt away. During these sessions, each family member has a chance to share his "truth" with the others. Following these moments, the pain subsides and real bonding occurs. Underneath all the hurt, anger and pain is love, understanding and forgiveness. The benefit of doing these sessions is that the focus in not on the SSA child but on family healing and reconciliation. The family healing sessions are held at the International Healing Foundation offices or in the family's home. We have several staff available to facilitate these family sessions.

About the Author

Richard Cohen, M.A., is one of the leading experts in the field of sexual reorientation and the author of *Coming Out Straight: Understanding and Healing Homosexuality, Alfie's Home* and *Gay Children, Straight Parents: A Plan for Family Healing.*

Cohen is the director of the International Healing Foundation (IHF), a non-profit organization he founded in 1990. Based in the Washington, D.C., area, IHF offers consultations/evaluations, teleconferencing classes, healing seminars, counselor training programs, and speaking engagements. As director Cohen travels extensively throughout the United States and Europe conducting seminars on marital relations, communication skills, parenting skills, sexual reorientation and healing from abuse and addictions. He is a frequent guest lecturer on college and university campuses, and at therapeutic and religious conferences.

Cohen holds a master's of arts degree in psychology from Antioch University and a bachelor's degree from Boston University. He has worked in child abuse treatment services, family reconciliation services, general counseling and support groups. For three years, he worked as an HIV/AIDS educator for the American Red Cross. He is the vice president and cofounder of Positive Alternatives To Homosexuality (PATH), an international coalition of organizations helping those with unwanted same-sex attractions (SSA).

As an expert in sexual reorientation—both as a coach and through his own personal experience transitioning from a homosexual to a heterosexual orientation in the 1980s—Cohen has been interviewed by newspaper, radio and television media, including appearances on *20/ 20*, *Larry King Live*, *The O'Reilly Factor*, *Paula Zahn Now* and *Jimmy Kimmel Live*.

Cohen lives in the Washington, D.C., metropolitan area with his wife and youngest son. His two adult children are making their mark in the world.